Enlightenment is Your Nature

Enlightenment is Your Nature

THE FUNDAMENTAL DIFFERENCE BETWEEN PSYCHOLOGY, THERAPY AND MEDITATION

OSHO

WATKINS

Sharing Wisdom Since
1893

This edition first published in the UK and USA 2017 by
Watkins, an imprint of Watkins Media Limited
19 Cecil Court
London WC2N 4EZ

enquiries@watkinspublishing.com

Design and typography copyright © Watkins Media Limited 2017

The material in this book is selected from various talks by
Osho given to a live audience. All of Osho's talks have been
published in full as books, and are also available as original audio
recordings. Audio recordings and the complete text archive can
be found via the online OSHO Library at www.osho.com

OSHO is a registered trademark of Osho International
Foundation, www.osho.com/trademarks.

1 3 5 7 9 10 8 6 4 2

Designed and typeset by JCS Publishing Services Ltd,
jcs-publishing.co.uk

Printed and bound by CPI Group (UK) Ltd, Croydon, CR0 4YY

A CIP record for this book is available from the British Library

ISBN: 978-1-78678-049-2

www.watkinspublishing.com

Contents

Preface

On the Neurosis of Becoming Human

Why is modern man so neurotic? It is because modern man is, for the first time, becoming human. The past of humanity is not that of human beings. Man has existed up to now as a crowd, not as individuals; man has existed in collectivities. The individual is being born; hence the modern man is very neurotic. It is a good indication; it is a great revolution that human consciousness is going through.

What is neurosis really? Neurosis is an indefinite state of mind, undecided, indecisive. To be this, or to be that? All outer definitions have disappeared, all props have been taken away. One's identity is very fragile – everyone knows it.

In the past it was very easy to answer the question, "Who am I?" Hindu, Christian, Mohammedan, Indian, Chinese, Tibetan, white/black, man/woman – things were clear, people knew who they were. Now it is not so clear; all those labels have disappeared. Everybody is standing nude, with no labels, and a great anxiety arises. Everybody has to define himself.

The work of defining oneself was done by others before – parents, teachers, priests, politicians. They were the authorities, the infallible authorities. You could be dependent easily; you did not need to think about things. Everything was chewed for you by others and given to you; you were spoon-fed.

Now man is becoming adult, mature. You have to work out your own identity. It is not so easy; only very intelligent people will be able to avoid neurosis. Utter intelligence will be needed; great silence, a great capacity to get out of the mind and its traps, will be needed in the future. And it will be needed more and more.

In the past, intelligence was not a great value – in fact, to be mediocre was more valuable. The mediocre person was always a fit with the society, and the talented person was always a misfit. No society in the past has ever liked people who were geniuses, because geniuses create trouble.

When a Buddha is alive he is a nuisance. His genuine intelligence disturbs the mediocre mind; his utter intelligence disturbs the stupid people. His individuality, his freedom, his rebellion hits hard on the mind of the crowd because the crowd does not want individuality. A crowd does not want uniqueness, the crowd simply wants to belong. It simply wants to be not responsible for anything. It wants to be part of a big crowd so the responsibility is always somewhere else – the Pope decides, the president decides, you need not bother about it. It is not for you to ask why, you are only to do and die.

In the modern mind is the first glimpse of individuality; hence, neurosis. In the past, all answers were fixed; one was not required to search for answers. God was there, heaven was there, the theory of karma was there, everything was so clear-cut; you could live with all those formulations very easily. Now you don't know; nothing is certain any more. A great paralysis is happening. This paralysis can either kill humanity or become a great, transforming, quantum leap.

I have heard that in a well-known experiment in learning theory, rats were trained to jump from a stand toward a pair of cards. There was a white card fixed in place – if the rats jumped toward it they fell to the ground. But if the rats jumped toward the other card, a black card, the card would fall and the rats could eat food that the experimenter had placed behind the card. The rats easily learned which card was which. If the cards were shifted around, they would learn to jump to the black card, wherever it happened to be.

But in the next stage of the experiment, the white and black cards were replaced by cards that successively approached a neutral grey. At some point the greys would become so similar that the rats could not distinguish between them. In this ambiguous situation, they refused to jump; they became almost paralysed, tense and neurotic.

This is the situation of man – a very potent situation, a pregnant situation. If people are just rats they will go really neurotic and they will commit suicide.

But man is not just a rat – notwithstanding what B F Skinner and other so-called psychologists say, man is not a rat. If there is a possibility that people might take this challenge and become more integrated, their neurosis will appear only in the interval. Sooner or later, they will know how to deal with it. Without authorities, without God, without Bibles and Vedas, they will fall upon their own consciousness. They will start functioning spontaneously, moment to moment, without any ready-made answers. Then the neurosis will disappear – and not only the neurosis, but the mob mind also. For the first time there will be beauty, grandeur, dignity.

In the past, man was not dignified. Yes, once in a while a Buddha happened, once in a while a Christ walked on the earth – but that was only once in a while. What about the millions of people who lived and died without knowing any taste of freedom, without ever knowing who they were? They believed they were Jews and died; they believed they were Hindus and died. They believed they were just their bodies and died. They never knew who they really were – they never came across the inner space. Unless you come across that inner space you live an undignified life. You live like rats and you will die like dogs.

To be human is risky. The risk is, you will have to pass through a kind of neurosis. Before you can become centred in your own being, you will have to go through a kind of un-centring. Zen people say: before you start meditating, mountains are mountains and rivers are rivers. When you meditate, when you go deep in meditation, mountains are no longer mountains and rivers are no longer rivers. But if you go on, if you persist and reach the highest peak of meditation, then again mountains are mountains and rivers are rivers.

This is one of the most significant statements ever made. In the middle, everything becomes confused.

This is a century of great transformation. Man will either fall back . . . and that is happening. That's why Adolf Hitler, Joseph Stalin, Benito Mussolini, Mao Zedong and people like these become so important. Why? Because they are authoritative; they say, "You don't know who you are? We will supply you with the answers." They are infallible people; they know everything. Adolf Hitler is absolutely certain; people start falling in line with him and they start following him.

The old gods have disappeared. It is very easy for Joseph Stalin or Mao Zedong to lead people because people cannot live without gods, people cannot live without priests. People cannot live on their own, this is the problem. So, during these past few decades man has seen two things happening: very few people have risen toward individuality and have become peaks like Everest. But many more have fallen back, have regressed and become fascists, communists, religious fundamentalists – and there are so many brands available.

And whenever a country is very confused, an Adolf Hitler is bound to arrive. It was not just an accident that Germany became a victim – one of the most intellectual countries in the world, a country of professors and scholars, thinkers and scientists. Why did a country of so many intelligent people become a victim of this madman? The reason was that these intelligent people – professors, philosophers – could not supply the ready-made answers. They were too polite, they were too hesitant, they were too humble, they were too intelligent. They could not shout, they only whispered – and people needed slogans, not whisperings.

Adolf Hitler shouted from the housetops. He was not whispering. He gave slogans – clear-cut, well defined. All that he gave is nonsense, but that is not the point. People are not worried about sense or nonsense, their whole thing is they want somebody who can shout so confidently that they can follow easily without any turmoil in their being. They followed Adolf Hitler.

It happens again and again in the history of man; intelligent people follow very unintelligent leaders. And this has been a problem for psychoanalysts: why does it happen? There is a reason for it. People who think, the more they think the more hesitant they become. They start talking in ifs and buts; they become humble. But people don't want humble statements. To the ordinary mind, a humble statement looks as if you are not certain, you don't know.

That's why, in India, Mahavir could not get many followers – and he was one of the most intelligent people that have ever walked on the earth. Why did it happen that he could not get followers? Compared to him, very ordinary people accumulated great masses of followers. What happened to Mahavir? The problem was that he was so humble. His statements always started with "perhaps". If you asked him "Is there a God?" he would say, "Perhaps." Who would follow such a man? You would think that he himself does not know. "Perhaps . . . maybe." Who is going to follow such a man? You ask him, "Is there a soul?" and he says, "Maybe." The natural inference is that he himself does not know.

The reality is just the opposite. He knows, and he knows so deeply that it can only be expressed by a perhaps, a maybe. It is so vast, it will be stupid to say yes or no – it will be reducing it to a very ordinary statement; it will become political. It will not have that height and plenitude of a philosophic experience.

"Yes, God is and God is not. God is both, and God is not both." In this way Mahavir used to talk. If you asked one question he would answer in seven ways. He would use all the categories of logic to answer your single question, but you would be left more puzzled than ever. You had come with one question and you would go with seven thousand questions. Who would follow this man?

Adolf Hitler says in his autobiography *Mein Kampf* that there is only one difference between truth and untruth, and the difference is of repetition. If you go on repeating an untruth loudly, forcibly, it becomes true. He experimented with the idea and he proved it to millions of people. Just utter nonsense, but he would go on repeating it and, slowly, people started believing in him. People needed a leader.

Nietzsche has said that God is no more. But people cannot live without God – they feel very shaky. So these are the two possibilities: either man will fall and become a victim of some kind of fascism, Nazism, communism, or – the second possibility, for which I am working – man may take this vagueness, which looks like neurosis, as a jumping-board. He may get free of the whole past and take a quantum leap into the future, and start living without leaders, without clinging, without any kind of belonging.

The whole earth is yours, it need not be divided. Christ and Buddha and Krishna are all yours, you need not be a Christian or a Hindu or a Mohammedan. The whole past is yours: use it, but don't be used by it. Use it, and go ahead. Use Buddha and Christ and Krishna and Zarathustra and Lao Tzu, but don't be confined by them. You have to go ahead. There is more to life, there are still unexplored realities. The mystery is infinite.

Man is in a kind of neurosis. This is a very pregnant situation: either you fall back or you jump ahead. Don't fall back. And falling back is not going to satisfy you, either. Only growth satisfies – regression, never. Even if your childhood looks very beautiful, it is not going to satisfy you if you become a child again. You will be miserable because you have known youth and the freedom of youth and the adventure of it. To be a child again, in the old sense that you were once a child, will not make you happy. You will feel reduced, not enhanced.

Man is in a kind of neurosis because being denied access to reality always produces insanity. By placing normal people in an abnormal situation, we get abnormal behavior. Modern man is a revving engine without clutches, wheels or destination. Old destinations are no longer relevant.

And man now has to learn something absolutely new, which has never been known before. Man now has to learn to live in the here-now. Yes, a sense of direction is needed, but not a fixed goal. A significance is needed, but not a definite meaning. A destiny is not needed – a dignity is needed, freedom is needed. Man has to explore his freedom and decide on his own.

Remember it: there is no given meaning, that's the problem. In the past there was a given meaning, you were told the meaning of life. Now nobody is telling you what your meaning of life is – you have to create it.

For the first time, man is on the verge of becoming a creator. Up to now you have been creatures – now you will be creators. History is taking a turn, you are on the threshold of a new consciousness.

Up to now man has lived like a creature – God was the creator and man was the creature. God was the one who decided, and man was the one who followed. Now this is going to be no longer the case. Now man is the creator, no longer the creature. Now man has to decide the meaning of his own life – he has to give significance to his own life with his own creativity. You cannot borrow it, you cannot beg it, you cannot bargain for it. You will have to create it . . . and this is really a problem! To create meaning needs great intelligence, to create meaning needs great awareness, to create meaning needs great endeavour.

People have learned a simple trick of begging. Somebody will give you meaning – your father, your mother or the Great Father in the skies. He will give you meaning, you just have to pray.

Gautam Buddha came 25 centuries before his time. Now is the time for him because he believes in freedom, he believes in individuality. He does not believe that you are creatures, he believes that you are creators. Buddha is going to become more and more relevant every day.

Create yourself. Give shape and form to your being. Paint your life, sculpt yourself. Whatever you will be, will be your work. It is not fate – you are responsible.

People don't want to be responsible; they are afraid of responsibility. They want somebody else to take care of them; they always need guardians. These are the people who are getting neurotic, because the guardians are no longer there. In fact they were never there; you believed in them and they were there only *because* you believed in them. Now the belief has disappeared, they have also disappeared. They were created by your belief.

Man has to learn to live alone on his own. This is a great opportunity – don't take it negatively, otherwise you will be in madhouses. Take it positively, accept the challenge and you will be the first real human beings on the face of the earth.

PART I

WHAT IS ENLIGHTENMENT?

Enlightenment is simply the process of becoming aware of your unconscious layers of personality and dropping those layers. They are not you; they are false faces. And because of those false faces, you cannot discover your original face.

Enlightenment is nothing but the discovery of the original face – the essential reality you brought with you, and the essential reality you will have to take with you when you die. All these layers gathered between birth and death will be left here behind you.

The man of enlightenment does exactly what death does to everybody, but he does it himself. He dies in a way and is reborn, dies in a way and is resurrected. And his originality is luminous because it is part of eternal life.

It is a simple process of discovering yourself.

You are not the container but the content.

Discarding the container and discovering the content is the whole process of enlightenment.

1

Paradise Regained

Man can live in two ways, the natural and the unnatural. The unnatural has great attraction in it because it is new, unfamiliar, adventurous. Hence, every child has to leave his nature and go into un-nature. No child can resist that temptation. To resist that temptation is impossible; the paradise has to be lost. The losing of it is built in; it can't be avoided, it is inevitable. And, of course, only man can lose it. That's man's ecstasy and agony, his privilege, his freedom and his fall.

Jean-Paul Sartre is right when he says that man is "condemned to be free". Why condemned? Because with freedom, choice arises – the choice of being natural or being unnatural. When there is no freedom there is no choice. Animals still exist in paradise; they never lose it. But because they never lose it, they can't be aware of it; they can't know where they are. To know where you are, you will have to lose it first. That's how knowing becomes possible – by losing.

You know a thing only when you have lost it. If you have never lost it, if it has always been there, you naturally take it for granted. It becomes so obvious that you become oblivious to it. Trees are still in paradise, and the mountains and the stars, but they don't know where they are. Only man can know. A tree can't become a buddha – not that there is any difference between the inner nature of a buddha and a tree, but a tree can't become a buddha. A tree is already a buddha! To become a buddha, the tree first has to lose its nature; it has to go away from it.

You can only see things from a certain perspective. If you are too close to them, you cannot see them. What Buddha has seen, no tree has ever seen. It is available to trees and to animals, but only Buddha becomes conscious of it – the paradise is regained. Paradise exists only when it is regained. Nature's beauties and mysteries are revealed only when you come back home. When you go against your nature, when you go furthest from yourself, only then one day does the return journey start. When you become thirsty for nature, when you start dying without it, you start returning.

This is the original fall. Man's consciousness is his original fall, his original sin. But without the original sin, there is no possibility of a Buddha or a Christ.

The first thing to be understood is that man can choose. He is the only animal in existence who can choose, who can do things that are not natural, who can do things that should not be done, who can go against himself and against existence, who can destroy himself and all his bliss – who can create hell. By creating hell, the contrast is created – and then one can see what heaven is. Only through the contrast is there a possibility to know.

So remember, there are two ways: one can live naturally or one can live unnaturally.

When I say one can live naturally, I mean one can live without improving upon oneself in any way. One can live in trust – that's what nature is. One can live in spontaneity. One can live without being a doer. One can live in inaction, what Taoists call *wei-wu-wei*, action through inaction. Nature means you are not to do anything; it is already happening. The rivers are flowing – not that they are doing something. And the trees are growing – not that they have to worry about it, not that they have to consult any guide for it. The trees are blooming

– not that they have to think and plan about the flowers, what colour they should be, what shape. It is all happening. The tree is blooming in a thousand flowers without a single worry, without a single thought, without a single projection, without any blueprint. It is simply blooming! Just as fire is hot, the tree grows. It is natural. It is in the very nature of things. The seed becomes the sprout, and the sprout becomes the plant, and the plant becomes the tree, and the tree one day is full of foliage, and then another day buds have started appearing, and the flowering and the fruits. And all that is simply *happening*.

The child growing in the mother's womb is not doing anything. He is in *wu-wei*. But it is not that nothing is happening. In fact, so much is happening that never again in life will so much happen. Those nine months in the mother's womb contain so much "happening" that if you live 90 years that much happening won't occur. Millions of things are happening. The child is conceived only as an invisible cell, and then things start happening, things start exploding. The child is not sitting there in that small cell like a little miniature person, thinking and planning and worrying and suffering from insomnia. There is nobody!

To understand this is to understand a man like Buddha – is to understand that things can happen without your ever being worried about them. Things have always already been happening. And even when you become a doer, you become a doer only on the surface. Deep down, things go on happening.

When you are fast asleep, do you think you are trying to breathe? It is happening. If a person had to breathe, had to remain constantly aware to breathe, nobody would ever be able to live, not even for a single day. One moment and you have forgotten, and it is gone. You forget to breathe in, and you are finished! Then how would you be able to go to sleep?

You will have to be constantly alert; you will have to wake yourself up many times in the night to see whether you are still breathing or not.

You eat food, and then you forget all about it. But millions of things are happening: the food is being digested, broken down, destroyed, changed, transformed chemically. It will become your blood, your bones, your marrow. Great work goes on. The blood is circulating continuously, throwing all the dead cells out of the body.

How much is going on within you without your doing at all?

Doing remains on the surface. Man can live on the surface in an artificial way, but deep down in the innermost core you are always natural. Your artificiality becomes simply a layer upon your nature. But the layer thickens every day – more thoughts, more plans, more activity, more doing. More of the doer, the ego . . . and a crust grows. And that is the crust Buddha calls *samsara*, world.

The phenomenon of the doer, of the ego . . . this is losing nature, going against nature, going away from nature. One day you have gone so far that you start feeling suffocated. You have gone so far that a kind of schizophrenia arises in your being. Your circumference starts falling apart from the centre. That is the point of conversion, the point when religion becomes relevant. The point when you start searching for a way out. The point where you start thinking, "Who am I?" The point where you start looking back: "From where am I coming? What is my original face? What is my nature? I have gone too far and now it is time to go back. One step more and I will fall apart. I have broken all the links; only a small bridge has remained."

All neurosis is nothing but this. That's why psychology itself cannot cure neurosis. It can give you beautiful explanations about it, it can satisfy you, console you, solace you; it can teach you how to live with your neurosis; it can help you not to worry too much about it. It can give you a pattern of life in which neurosis can exist and you can also exist – it can teach you a kind of co-existence. But it cannot dissolve it – only meditation can dissolve it. And unless psychology takes a quantum leap and becomes a support for meditation, it will remain partial.

Why can meditation cure the neurosis? Why can meditation cure schizophrenia? Because it can make you one whole. The circumference is no longer against the centre; they are holding hands, they are embracing each other. They are one. They function in one rhythm, they vibrate as one vibration. That is real health – and wholeness, and holiness. That's where buddhahood arises – a person has become sane again.

Unless you are a buddha you will remain insane, more or less. Insanity is bound to remain a part of your being. You can manage to live with it somehow, but it is going to be just "somehow". It is a management, you cannot relax about it.

Have you not observed? Everybody is afraid of going mad. One keeps oneself in control, but the fear is always there: "If something goes wrong, if one thing more goes wrong, then I may not be able to control myself any longer." Everybody is on the verge of it. People are just about 99 per cent on the verge. One per cent more, any small thing, the last straw on the camel – the bank fails, your partner leaves and escapes with somebody else, the business dwindles – and you are no longer sane, all sanity gone. It must have been just a facade, that sanity that goes so easily. It must have been very thin, fragile.

In fact, it was not there.

The change between the ordinary person and the insane is only of quantity, not of quality. Unless you become a Buddha or a Christ or a Krishna – these are all names of the same state of consciousness, where centre and circumference function in a dance, in a symphony – unless that symphony arises, you will remain phony, you will remain false, you will remain arbitrary, you will not really have a soul. And it is not that you *cannot* have it – it is always yours; just for the asking you will have it. Jesus says, "Knock and the door shall be opened unto you. Ask and it shall be given" – just for the asking, and you will get it.

But there is great attraction in the unnatural, because the unnatural is alien, the unnatural is opposite to you, and the opposite always attracts. The opposite always intrigues, the opposite is always there as a challenge. You would like to know . . .

That's why a man becomes interested in a woman, a woman becomes interested in a man. That's how people become interested and attracted to each other, because the other is the opposite. And the same rule follows deep down. Your natural being seems to be already yours, so what is the point of getting hold of it, of being it? One wants something new.

That which you have you lose all interest in. That's why you are missing godliness, because godliness you already have and you cannot be interested in it. You are interested in the world, in money, in power and prestige – those things you don't have. Godliness is already given – and by godliness I mean nature. Who bothers about nature? Why think about it when in the first place you already have it? We are interested in that which we don't have, and the unnatural attracts. One becomes focused on the unnatural and the artificial, and one rushes into it. From one unnatural style of life into another unnatural style of life.

And remember, not only are the so-called worldly people unnatural, the so-called religious are also unnatural. That is the great understanding that Buddha brings to the world – and that understanding has become a ripe fruit in Zen. That is the fundamental contribution of Buddha.

A man remains artificial in the so-called world – earning money, power, prestige. And then one day he becomes religious, but again he is moving into another kind of unnaturalness. Now he practices yoga, stands on his head – all stuff and nonsense. What are you doing there, standing on your head? Can't you stand on your feet? But to stand on your feet seems so natural that it has no attraction.

When you see somebody standing on his head, you think, "Yes, he is doing something. Here is a real man." You are attracted – he must be gaining something that you have not known yet, and you would also like to practice it. People start doing all kinds of stupid things, but those are all again the same. The pattern is the same, the gestalt is the same. The change is very slight. The quality is the same.

You were earning money; now you are more interested in heaven, the next life. You were interested in what people think about you; now you are interested in what God thinks about you. You were interested in making a beautiful house here; now you are interested in making a beautiful house in paradise, in the other world. You were being unnatural, you were eating too much; now you start fasting.

Just see how one changes from one unnatural attitude to another unnatural attitude. You were eating too much, you were obsessed with eating, you were continuously stuffing yourself, then one day you are fed up with this – literally fed up with this – so you start fasting. Now again, a thrill arises in you. Now again you can hope that something is going to happen. And you can go to the extreme of fasting, which is as much against nature as eating too much.

To be natural is just in the middle. Buddha has called his way The Middle Way – because the natural exists just exactly in the middle between opposite extremes.

You have been chasing women your whole life, and then one day you decide to become a celibate and move to a Catholic monastery, or become a Hindu monk and go to the Himalayas. This is the same person who was continuously chasing women; now he is tired of it, now he wants to drop it absolutely. Now he wants to move in the opposite direction; he escapes into a monastery. Now he enforces celibacy on himself, which is as unnatural as the first attitude. But one unnaturalness leads to another and one can go on in circles . . . Beware of it.

To be natural has no appeal, because to be natural means your ego will not be satisfied in any way. And a man like Buddha is preaching only one single thing: to be ordinary, to be nobody, to be natural.

The natural person is the enlightened person. To be natural is to be enlightened. To be as natural as animals and trees and stars, to have no imposition upon oneself, to have no idea of how one should be, is to be enlightened. Enlightenment is a state of being natural. It is not something like an achievement.

When you think of enlightenment you always think of it as an achievement. People come to me and they ask, "Osho, how are we going to achieve enlightenment?" It is not a state of achievement – because whatsoever you achieve or you can achieve will be artificial. The natural need not be achieved: it is already there! It has never been otherwise.

You are not to achieve enlightenment, you are simply to drop that achieving mind. You have to relax into it. It is available – from the very beginning it is available. Relax into it.

An enlightened person is not somebody who has reached to the pinnacle, who has reached the topmost rung of the ladder. You are all ladder-climbers. You need a ladder – it may be in the marketplace or in the monastery, it makes no difference, but you need a ladder. You carry your ladders with you. Wherever you can find a place, you simply set up your ladder and start climbing. Nobody even asks, "Where are you going? Where is this ladder going to lead you?" But after one rung there is another rung, and you are curious: "Maybe something is there!" So you go one step more. Another rung is waiting for you, and you become curious and you start moving.

That's how people move in the world of money, that's how people move in the world of politics. And it is not only that you have to move – because many people are going on the same ladder, you have to push others back. You have to pull on their legs, you have to make a place for yourself, you have to make space for yourself; you have to be aggressive, you have to be violent. And when there is so much violence and so many people fighting, who bothers where you are going? You must be going *somewhere* if so many other people are interested.

And if you become too much of an enquirer, you will lose the race. So there is no time to think about it, to enquire, "What is the point of it all?" Enquirers are losers, so one has not to think. One has just to rush and go on rushing. And the ladder is non-ending – rung upon rung, rung upon rung. The mind can go on projecting new rungs. And when you move into a monastery the same continues. Now a spiritual hierarchy is there, and you start moving in that hierarchy. You become very serious, and the same competitiveness comes in.

This is just an ego game. And ego can play its game only in the artificial. Wherever you see a ladder, beware – you are in the same trap!

Enlightenment is not the last rung of a ladder. Enlightenment is getting down from the ladder, getting down forever and never asking for any ladder again, becoming natural.

I have to use the word "becoming" which is not true. It should not be used, but that's how language is – it is made by those ladder-climbers. You cannot become natural because whatsoever you *become* will be unnatural. Becoming is unnatural – *being* is natural. So, forgive me, I have to use the same language, a language that is not meant to be used for something natural. So you have to understand it. Don't be caught by the words.

When I say become natural, I am simply saying to stop becoming, and fall, relax into being. You are already there!

Why do people go on moving in circles?

First, they have become very skilful in it. And nobody wants to drop his skill, because the skill gives you a feeling of confidence, it gives you a feeling of strength. There are millions of people in the world who go on in the same rut again and again because they have become skilful. If they change, in the new space they may not be so skilful – they will not be. So they go on running in the circle – and they go on being bored, more and more bored. But the more they move in the circle the more skilful they become. Then they can't stop themselves. And they can't stop because of others too, because others are rushing by. If they stop they will be defeated. It is really a mad world.

Then too, one feels good repeating the same thing again and again. Monotony is consoling. People who are bewildered and frightened by too much change find relief in monotony.

That's why teenagers like the beat of certain types of music, and why some mental patients repeat the same act or word, over and over. You can go and watch people in a mental asylum, and you will be surprised that so many of the mad people have their mantras. Somebody is washing his hands continuously – day in, day out, just washing his hands. It is his mantra. It keeps him engaged, it keeps him occupied, it keeps him unafraid. And he knows how to do it; it is a simple act. If he stops doing it he becomes frightened – nothing to hang on to. If he stops doing it, he is empty – nothing to cling to. If he stops doing it, he does not know who he is. He has his identity as the hand-washer. He knows himself perfectly well when he is washing his hands, who he is. Once he stops it, difficulties arise.

In the mental asylum, those people who have devised their own mantras – in action, in words – are just consoling themselves. This is the whole secret of transcendental meditation and its success in America. America is today a great mental asylum. It needs something to repeat, monotonously, continuously. It helps people – just the same gesture, the same posture, the same mantra. You know that territory perfectly well; you go on moving in it, and it keeps you away from yourself.

Transcendental meditation is not meditation, and it is not transcendental either. It is just a consolation. It keeps you unaware of your insanity. Only an insane person can be convinced to repeat a mantra, otherwise not.

So people go on doing the same thing that they have done down the ages, in so many lives. Just watch yourself: you fall in one love, then in another, then in another . . . this is transcendental meditation, the same act. And you know that first time it was frustration, second time it was

13

frustration, third time it was frustration – and you know beforehand that the fourth time also it is going to be frustration. But you don't want to see it, you don't want to look into it, because if you look into it then you are left alone with nothing to do.

That falling in love keeps you engaged, keeps you on the run, keeps you moving. At least you can avoid yourself, you can escape from yourself. You need not look into the deepest question: who are you? You know that you are a great lover, so you go on counting how many women you have been involved with. There are people who keep count; they go on keeping count: 360, 361, 362. They have not loved a single woman. And there are people who keep count of their mantras, how many times they repeat the mantra. There are people who go on writing in their books: *Rama, Rama, Rama* . . . they go on writing it.

Once I stayed in a man's house. I was surprised, the whole house was a great library. I asked, "What kind of scriptures do you have?"

He said, "Only one kind of scripture: I go on writing "Rama, Rama, Rama" – that's my mantra. From the morning to the evening I do only one thing; I have written it millions of times, and these are all my records." And that man was respected very much in his town. Now, he is just a madman, utterly mad! If he is stopped from doing this nonsense, he will immediately go mad. This mad activity was keeping him in some way sane.

Ninety-nine per cent of your religion is nothing but a device to keep you somehow sane.

A buddha is a totally different kind of person. He is the arch-enemy of showbiz. He is somebody who wants to tell the truth, and *as it is* he wants to tell it. He shatters all rubbish religious ideologies. He simply shocks you to the very roots. And if you are available he can become a door – a door back home; a door, a threshold, that can make you able to fall back into nature.

In every complicated culture, in every complicated civilization, there are professional liars and professional truth-tellers, but they are not very different; they are the same people. The professional liars are called lawyers, and the professional truth-tellers are known as priests. They simply repeat scriptures.

A buddha is neither a liar nor a professional truth-teller. He simply makes his heart available to you; he wants to share. Hence, the whole Indian priesthood was against Gautam Buddha. He was thrown out of his own country. His temples were burnt, his statues were destroyed. Many Buddhist scriptures are available now only in Chinese or Tibetan translations. The originals are lost; they must have been burnt.

Thousands of Buddhists were killed in the non-violent country of India. They were burnt alive. Buddha shocked the professional truth-tellers very deeply. He was bent upon destroying their whole business. He simply made it an open secret.

Listen to these words of Ikkyu. They describe Buddha's approach profoundly.

> Of heaven or hell we have
> No recollection, no knowledge;
> We must become what we were
> Before we were born.

Everything finally returns to its source. That's the law of nature. Nature moves in a perfect circle, so everything has to return to its source. Knowing the source, you can know the goal – because the goal can never be other than the source.

You plant a seed, and then the tree arises. Years it will take, and the tree will spread its wings in the sky and will have dialogues with the stars, and will live a long life . . . and finally what happens? The tree produces seeds again and the seeds fall into the earth and again new trees arise. It is a simple movement.

The source is the goal!

Your body will fall back into the earth and will become part of the earth because it comes from the earth. Your breath will disappear into air because it comes from the air. The water that is in your body will go back to the sea; that's where it comes from. The fire that is in you will go into fire. And the consciousness that is in you will move into the consciousness of the whole. Everything goes back to its source.

This fundamental has to be remembered – because by knowing it, by understanding it, you drop all other goals, because then all other goals are arbitrary.

Somebody says, "I want to become a doctor, an engineer, a scientist, a poet" – these are all artificial goals that you have fixed upon yourself. The natural goal is the innocence that you had in your mother's womb. Or go even deeper . . . the nothingness from where you came, that is the natural goal. And to live naturally means to know this; otherwise, you are bound to create some artificial goal.

Somebody wants to become enlightened – that is an artificial goal. I am not saying that people don't become enlightened, but I am saying don't make it a goal. People become enlightened only when they have fallen back to their original source; when they have become natural they are enlightened.

If this is understood through meditations, through your own inner search, then you will never choose any artificial goal. All artificial goals lead you astray. Then one starts relaxing into nature; one becomes one's original nature; one becomes one's originality. And in that originality, in that ordinary naturalness, is buddhahood, is enlightenment.

Shunryo Suzuki, one of the first Zen masters to live and teach in the West, was once asked why he never spoke much about **satori**, *enlightenment. The master laughed and answered, "The reason I do not talk about* **satori** *is because I have never had it." What did he mean?*

Zen in the West operates in a very strange context. The master you are talking about, Shunryo Suzuki, must have felt immense difficulty to express himself, because Zen has a language of its own. It has a climate different from any other climate that exists on the earth.

To bring Zen to any country is a difficult task. One has to be ready to be misunderstood. Suzuki's statement seems to be clear, and anybody who reads it will not appear to have any difficulty understanding it. But whatever he understands will be wrong.

The master was asked, "Why don't you speak about *satori*?" – the Japanese word for enlightenment. And Suzuki answered the way a Zen master should answer, knowing perfectly well that he could not be understood, that he was bound to be misunderstood. He said, "The reason I do not talk about *satori* is because I have never had it."

The statement is clear; linguistically there is no problem, there seems to be nothing unclear in it. Suzuki is saying, "I have never talked about it because I have never had it." Now

I will have to give you the whole background, the climate in which the meaning of the sentence turns into exactly the opposite of what you understand by it.

Zen has an absolute certainty that no one can have *satori* or enlightenment; you can have *things*. You can have money, you can have power, you can have the whole world, but you cannot have enlightenment.

Enlightenment is not a thing; it is not possible to possess it. Those who say they have it, don't have it – they don't even understand the ABC of it. One *becomes* enlightened – that's what Suzuki is saying. There is no distinction between "I" and enlightenment, so how can I *have* it? The "I" disappears completely into enlightenment just like a dewdrop disappearing in the ocean. Can the dewdrop say, "I have the ocean"? The dewdrop *is* the ocean; there is no question of having it. This is the first thing to be clearly understood.

Suzuki was an enlightened master; that's why he denied it. If he were not enlightened but only a scholar, learned about Zen, he might have felt embarrassed to deny it. He might rather have lied, and nobody would have been able to detect his lie. He could have said, "I have it, but the experience is inexpressible; it was so simple, that's why I never talk about it." But the man *really* had it. To really have it means you can't have it; you disappear.

As long as you are, there is no enlightenment.

The moment there is enlightenment, you are not. You disappear just like darkness disappears when there is light. Darkness cannot possess light, and you cannot possess enlightenment.

I don't think that the statement of Suzuki would have been understood by the people who asked the question, and received the right answer. It needs a totally different context to understand.

The Western education is so much of a nourishment to the ego. In fact, Western psychology supports the idea that a person should have a very clear ego – powerful, aggressive, ambitious; otherwise, one cannot survive in the struggle of existence. To survive, first you have to be. And you not only have to be defensive, it is taught that the right way of defence is to offend, to attack. Before anybody else attacks you, you should attack. You should be the first, not the second, because to be defensive is already losing the battle.

Because of the Western psychology, the whole educational system supports the idea that a man becomes mature as he attains a more and more crystallized ego. This goes against the experience of all the buddhas, of all the awakened ones. And none of these psychologists or educationalists have any glimpse of what awakening is, of what enlightenment is.

Those who have become enlightened are agreed, without any exception, on the point that the ego has to disappear. It is false, it is created by society; it is not your original face, it is not you. The false must disappear for the real to be.

So remember these steps: first, the false must disappear for the real to be, and then the real has to disappear into the ultimately real. People are living so far away from their ultimate home – they are not even real, what to say about the ultimate? For that, they have to first move away from the ego. They have to experience in meditation their own centre.

But this is not the end. Meditation is only a beginning of the journey. In the end, the seeker is dissolved in the sought, the knower in the known, the experiencer in the experience. Who is going to have *satori*? You are absent; you are non-existent when enlightenment explodes. Your absence is an absolute necessity for enlightenment to happen.

Suzuki is absolutely right: "The reason I do not talk about *satori* is because I have never had it." And I am absolutely certain that those who heard him are bound to have thought that he had had no experience of *satori*. That is simply the literal meaning of what he is saying. Unless there was somebody in his audience who had experienced egolessness, and finally selflessness, Suzuki was, without fail, bound to be misunderstood.

But he was a man of immense daring, of great courage, to introduce Zen to the West. Not many people were impressed. Many certainly entertained Suzuki's statements, his anecdotes from the annals of Zen. They thought them strange jokes. But there were a few who understood not what the man was saying, but the man himself. He turned a few people on; he has the same distinction as Bodhidharma, who planted the seeds of Zen in China.

Suzuki can be compared to Bodhidharma. He planted the seeds in the West and Zen became, in the Western climate and mind, a new fashion. Suzuki was very much disturbed by it. He was not introducing a new fashion, he was introducing a new revolution and a new style of being. But the West understands things only in that way – every two or three years a new fashion is needed; people become bored with the old.

Suzuki was received with joy because he had brought something that no Christian or Jew was even able to comprehend. He attracted many people of the younger generation; a few of them remained true to the master to the very end. Many travelled to Japan just because of Suzuki. Hundreds of Zen classics were translated into Western languages because of Suzuki. Now it is possible to talk about Zen and still be understood, and the whole credit goes to a single man, Shunryo Suzuki.

It has never to be forgotten that words don't exist without context. If you forget the context, whatever you will understand is going to be wrong. If you understand the context, it is impossible to misunderstand.

Berkowitz was crossing Washington Avenue on Miami Beach when he was hit by a passing auto. Several passers-by picked him up and laid him down on a bench. A kindly, silver-haired lady approached the injured man and asked, "Are you comfortable?"

"Ehhh! I make a living," sighed Berkowitz.

In his own context, Berkowitz could not understand the word "comfortable" in any sense other than that of making a good living. He has had an accident, but he cannot understand the word "comfortable" in that context. Perhaps he may be dying, perhaps he is badly hurt, but his context remains within his old mind.

This has to be remembered while you are studying Zen – the differences of context.

I understand you to say that enlightenment is the transcendence of mind – conscious, unconscious, sub-conscious – and that one dissolves into the ocean of life, into the universe, into nothingness. I also hear you talking about the individuality of human beings. How can the individuality of an enlightened person manifest itself if he is dissolved in the whole?

The ordinary, unconscious human being has no individuality; he has only a personality.

Personality is that which is given by others to you – by the parents, by the teachers, by the priest, by the society –

whatever they have said about you. And you have been desiring to be respectable, to be respected, so you have been doing things which are appreciated, and the society goes on rewarding you, respecting you more and more. This is their method of creating a personality.

But personality is very thin, skin-deep. It is not your nature. The child is born without a personality, but he is born with a potential individuality. The potential individuality simply means his uniqueness from anybody else – he is different.

So first, remember that individuality is not personality. When you drop personality, you discover your individuality – and only the individual can become enlightened. The false cannot become the ultimate realization of truth. Only the true can meet with the true, only the same can meet the same. Your individuality is existential; hence when your individuality blossoms you become one with the whole. Here is the question: if you become one with the whole, then how can you remain individual?

The problem is simply a non-understanding. The experience of becoming the whole is of consciousness, and the expression of it is through the body, through the mind. The experience is beyond the body–mind structure. When one becomes absolutely silent, goes into *samadhi*, reaches the fourth stage ... he is not body, he is not mind. They are all silent – he is far above them. He is pure consciousness.

This pure consciousness is universal, just as this light in all the bulbs in this room is one, but it can be expressed differently. The bulb can be blue, the bulb can be green, the bulb can be red; the shape of the bulb can be different. The body–mind are still there, and if the man of experience wants to express his experience, then he has to use the body–mind;

there is no other way. And his body–mind are unique – only he has that structure, nobody else has that structure.

So he has experienced the universal, he has become the universal, but to the world, to the others, he is a unique individual. His expression is going to be different from other realized people. It is not that he wants to be different; he has a different mechanism, and he can only come through that mechanism to you.

There have been enlightened painters. They have never spoken because word was not their art, but they have painted. And their paintings are totally different from ordinary paintings, even of the great masters. Even the greatest master painters are unconscious people; what they paint reflects their unconsciousness.

But if a realized man paints, then his painting has a totally different beauty. It is not only a painting, it is a message too. It has a meaning to be discovered. The meaning has been given in code, because the man was capable only of painting, so his painting is a code. You have to discover the code, and then the painting will reveal immense meanings. The deeper you go into those meanings, the more and more you will find. The other paintings are just flat; they may be made by masters, but they are flat. The paintings made by a realized man are multi-dimensional, they are not flat. They want to say something to you. If the man is a poet, like Kabir, then he sings, and his poetry is his expression.

If the man is articulate in speaking the unspeakable, then he speaks; but his words will have a totally different impact. The same words are used by everybody, but they don't have that impact because they don't carry the same energy, they don't come from the same sourcc. A man of experience brings his words full of his experience – they are not dry, they are not the words of an orator or a speaker. He may not know the art of speaking but no orator can do what he can do with words. He can transform people just by their hearing him. Just by being in the presence of him, just by letting his words rain over you, you will feel a transformation happening: a new being is born in you, you are reborn.

So when I say that even enlightened people have individuality, I mean that they remain unique – for the simple reason that they have a unique body–mind structure, and anything that comes to you has to come through that structure.

Buddha speaks in one way, Mahavira speaks in another way. Chuang Tzu speaks in absurd stories – he is a great storyteller – but his stories, side by side, go on playing with your heart. The stories are so absurd that your mind cannot do anything. That's the reason why he has chosen the stories to be absurd, so that your mind cannot come in between. With his absurd stories he stops your mind, and then his presence is available to you and to your heart; you can drink the wine he has brought for you. And he has put your mind away by telling you an absurd story. The mind is puzzled and is not functioning.

Many people have wondered why Chuang Tzu writes such absurd stories, but nobody has been able to explain the fact for the simple reason that the people who have been thinking about why he is writing the stories have no idea that it is a device to make the mind stop functioning – then you are available, fully available from your heart. He can contact you in that way.

But Buddha cannot tell an absurd story. He uses parables, but they are very meaningful. He does not want to avoid the mind . . . these are the uniquenesses of the people. He wants the mind to be convinced and then, through that conviction of the mind, he wants to go to your heart. If the mind is convinced it gives way. And Buddha's parables, his discourses, are all logical; the mind has to give way sooner or later.

Different masters . . . For example, Jalaluddin Rumi did nothing but whirling. He became enlightened after 36 hours of continuous whirling, without any stop – non-stop whirling. In fact every child likes to whirl. Parents stop him; they say, "You will fall. You may have a fit or you may get hit by something – don't do such a thing." But all children all over the world love whirling, because somehow while the child is whirling he finds his centre. Without finding the centre you cannot whirl. The body goes on whirling, but the whirling has to happen on a centre; so slowly, slowly he becomes aware of the centre.

After 36 hours of continuous whirling, Rumi became absolutely clear about his centre. That was his experience of the ultimate, the fourth. Then his whole life he was not doing anything but teaching whirling to people. It will look absurd to a Buddhist, it will look absurd to any other religion – because, what can you get out of whirling? It is a simple method, the simplest method, but it may suit you or it may not.

For example, for me it does not suit. I cannot sit on a swing, that is enough to create nausea in me. And what to say about sitting myself on a swing? – I cannot see somebody else swinging! That is enough to give me a feeling of nausea. Now, Rumi is not for me. And there may be many people to whom whirling will give nausea, vomiting. That means it is not for them.

We are individually different. And there is no contradiction. One can experience the universal, and yet when the question of expression arises, one has to be individual.

Peeling the Onion of Personality

Understanding Your Conditioning

Man is like an onion, exactly like an onion, with layers and layers of personality; and behind all those layers is hidden the essence. That essence is like emptiness, void. It is more like non-being than like being, because being has a limitation, a boundary to it. But that innermost core has no boundary to it, it has no limitation, it is just a freedom, a free flow of energy, infinite in its dimensions.

Unless one goes on peeling one's layers of personality to the very end, and rediscovers the essence, one remains sickminded. Sickmindedness is being stuck somewhere, frozen somewhere. Sickmindedness is being blocked. It is an impasse – it is exactly how the word *impasse* sounds, you cannot pass through it. You are blocked. You do not have the freedom to flow, to be and not to be. You are forced to be *something*. You are more like a solid rock than like a river.

Freedom is health. Being blocked, stuck, is sickmindedness – and everybody, almost everybody, is sick. Rarely does it happen that one gathers courage to penetrate to the very innermost core of non-being. Then one becomes a buddha – whole, healthy, holy.

We have to understand these layers of personality because the very understanding is a healing force. If you understand exactly where you are blocked, the blocks start melting. This is the miracle of understanding a thing – the very understanding helps it to melt. Nothing else needs to be done. If you really, exactly know – if you can pinpoint where you are blocked, where you are frozen, where the impasse exists – then just being aware of it, knowing it in its totality, starts it melting. Knowing is a healing force, and once it starts melting you again regain the flow. You become flowing.

The first layer of your personality is the most superficial – the layer of formalities, social niceties. It is needed; nothing is wrong in it. You meet a person on the road, you know the person. If you don't say anything, and he also doesn't say anything, if no social formality is fulfilled, you both feel embarrassed. Something has to be done. Not that you mean it, but it is a social lubricant; so the first layer I call the layer of the lubricant. It supports smoothness. It is the layer of, "Good morning, how are you? Great! Fine! Nice weather! Well, be seeing you." This layer is good, nothing is wrong in it; if you use it, it is beautiful. But if you are *used by* it, and you have become frozen in it and you have lost all contact with your innermost being, if you never move beyond this layer, then you are stuck. You are sickminded.

It is beautiful to say "Good morning" to somebody, but a person who never says more than that is ill. He has no contact with life. In fact, these formalities are not a lubricant to him; on the contrary, they have become a means of withdrawal, an avoidance. You see somebody, you say "Good morning" to avoid the person so that you can go on your own way and escape from him.

This social formality has become a frozen thing with millions of people; they live on this layer and never move beyond it. Etiquette, manners, words, chatter, always on the surface – they talk not to communicate, they talk to avoid communication. They talk to avoid the embarrassing situation in which you encounter the other. They are closed people. If their life is a misery it is no wonder. If they live in hell, it is not surprising. In fact, they are dead people.

The founder of gestalt therapy, Fritz Perls, used to call this layer the "chicken shit" layer, dead, dry. Many people live in chicken shit. Their whole life is just a useless formality. They move nowhere, they are stuck at the door; they have not entered the chamber of life. Life has many chambers and they are just standing at the door, on the steps. Steps are good if you step over them; they are dangerous if you start clinging to them.

So remember, a healthy person uses the layer of social formality; then it is a lubricant, it is beautiful. An unhealthy person makes it his whole life – smiles and does not mean it, laughs and does not mean it. If somebody dies he becomes sad, cries, even tears flow from his eyes . . . but it is all false! He does not mean it. He never means anything. He is just continuously on show, continuously on display. His whole life is just an exhibition. He cannot enjoy it because he cannot move withinwards.

Formality is not a relationship. It can help, or it can hinder. A healthy person uses it to go deeper; an unhealthy person becomes stuck in it. You can see those people all around, smiling . . . in Lions Clubs, Rotary Clubs. Chicken-shit people – always well-dressed, groomed, looking perfectly okay, and absolutely wrong. Completely ill, utterly unhealthy and just putting on a show. This becomes a fixed pattern with them. When they come back from the Rotary Club or the Lions Club they talk to their children but just on the same level. They make love to their wives but just on the same level. Their whole life is a string of mannerisms. Books on etiquette are their Bibles, Gitas and Korans, and they think if they fulfil whatsoever is required of them by the society, they have achieved something.

This layer has to be broken. Remain aware that you don't get caught in it. Remain aware, and if you are stuck at this level, become aware – the very awareness will help the block to melt, evaporate, and energy will become available to enter into the second layer.

The second layer is that of roles and games. The first layer has no contact with life. The second layer sometimes can have glimpses. In the second layer are, "I am the husband, you are the wife." Or, "I am the wife, you are the husband; I am the father, you are the child." Or, "I am the President of the United States, the Queen of England" – all the politicians of the world live on the second, the layer of role playing. Everybody goes on thinking that he or she is the greatest in the world – the greatest man in the world, the greatest poet, the greatest philosopher, greatest this and that . . .

The layer of the ego is the second layer. You go on playing roles and you continually have to change your role. You are sitting in your room and the servant enters; you change to the role of the master, the bully. You look at the servant as if he is not a human being. You are the boss and the servant is a nonentity. Then *your* boss enters – suddenly the role changes. Now you are nobody, you are wagging your tail; the boss has come and you are standing up to greet him. Continually, 24 hours a day in each relationship you have a different role to play. There is nothing wrong in it, it is a beautiful drama – if you are not stuck in it. It needs to be played, life *is* a great drama. In the East we have called it *leela*, the play of the divine. It is a play; one has to play many roles but one need not become fixed in any role.

29

One should remain always free of all roles; roles should be like clothes – you can at any time jump out of them. If that capability is retained, then you are not stuck; then you can play a role – there is nothing wrong in it! As far as it goes it is beautiful, but if it becomes your life and you don't know anything beyond it, then it is dangerous. Then you go on playing a thousand and one games in life and you never come in contact with life itself.

Fritz Perls calls it the layer of bullshit. It is a very big layer. Many people are caught in it; up to the neck they are full of bullshit. They carry the whole burden of the world, as if the whole world depends on them. If they do not exist, what will happen to the world? There will be chaos! Everything will be destroyed if they are not there – they are holding everything in place. These people are sick.

People of the first type, who live only in the first layer, are absolutely sick but they are not very dangerous. The second layer of people are not so absolutely sick, but they are more dangerous because they become the politicians, the generals, the power-holders, millionaires. They accumulate money and power and prestige and this and that, and they play great games. Because of their games, millions of people are not allowed even a glimpse of life; millions are sacrificed because of their games.

If you are stuck in the second layer, become alert. Remember always there are two possibilities at every level. The first layer is a lubricant for one who understands it; there is nothing wrong in it, it helps. It smooths the ability to move in the world. Millions of people are around, much conflict exists – this is bound to be, and if you are a little formal with people and you know how to behave, it helps. It helps you and it helps others also; there is nothing wrong in it. But if this first layer becomes the whole thing, then everything goes wrong. Then the medicine becomes the poison. This distinction has to be remembered continuously on every level.

On the second level, if you are just enjoying the game, knowing well that this is a game and you are not serious about it . . . The moment you become serious it is no longer a game; it has become the reality and then you are caught. If you enjoy it as fun, it is perfectly good! Enjoy it and help others to enjoy it; the whole world is a great stage, but don't be serious about it. Seriousness means illness has entered into your being. Now you think this is the whole, that becoming President of the United States is all. You sacrifice yourself and others and you use all sorts of means to achieve this end . . . and when it is fulfilled you find that nothing is fulfilled! Because it was just on the game layer, a dream thing, and when you awake you are deeply frustrated – your whole life gone, nothing achieved.

This is the frustration of rich people. This is the frustration of affluent countries. This is the frustration of all those who become successful. When they succeed, then they suddenly fail. Then they come face to face with the fact that they have wasted their life in a game. Remember, be alert – otherwise, if you are not stuck at the first layer you can be stuck at the second.

Then there is a third layer, the layer of chaos. Because of this third layer people are afraid to move inwards; that's why they get stuck in the second layer.

In the second layer everything is clean, clear. The rules are known, because every game has its rules. If you know the rules, you can play the game. Nothing is mysterious in the second layer. Two plus two always make four in the second layer – not so in the third. The third is not like the second,

31

it is chaos – tremendous energy, with no rules. You become afraid. The third layer gives you fear.

That's why when you start meditating, and you fall from the second layer to the third, you feel chaos. Suddenly, you don't know who you are! The world of "who is who" is the second, the bullshit layer. If you want to know about the second, go and consult a *Who's Who* book. They are published all over the world, and the names of the people in those books are people of the second layer.

In the third layer suddenly you become aware that you don't know who you are. Identity is lost, rules disappear, tremendous chaos arises, a vast ocean in a storm. It is beautiful if you can understand. If you cannot understand, it is really terrible. This third layer – if understood well, and if you can remain mindful in it – will give you the first glimpse, the first vital glimpse of life. Otherwise you will go neurotic.

In the third layer, people go mad. They are more honest than the people who belong to the first and second layers – a person who has gone mad has simply dropped formalities, has dropped role playing, and has allowed chaos to envelop him. He is better than your politicians; at least he is more sincere and truer to life.

I'm not saying to go and become neurotics, go and become mad, but madness happens at the third layer. All great artists belong to the third layer, and all great artists are prone to go mad. A Van Gogh goes mad; why? Artists, musicians, poets, painters – they belong to the third layer. They are sincere people, more sincere than your politicians, than your so-called monks, popes, mahatmas – these all belong to the second layer, playing a role, for example, of being a mahatma. The third layer is of more sincere and honest people, but there is a danger: they are so sincere and honest that they fall into chaos. They don't cling to the world of rules, and then they are in the storm.

If one can remain alert in the third layer, aware, meditative, then that chaos turns into a cosmos. It is chaos only because you are not centred, not aware. If you are aware it becomes a cosmos, an order . . . and not the order of human rules. It is the order of Tao, the order of what Buddha called the *dharma*. It is the ultimate order, not the man-made order. And if you remain alert, the chaos is there but you are not in the chaos – you transcend it. Awareness is a transcending phenomenon; you know that all around is chaos, but deep within you there is no chaos. Suddenly you are above it; you are not lost in it.

Poets, painters, musicians get lost in it because they don't know how to be aware. But they are more honest people. In the madhouses of the world there are more honest people than in the capitals of the world, and if I were allowed my way I would turn capitals into madhouses!

People in madhouses need help to go beyond the third to the fourth. Sufis have a particular word for the third-layer people; they call them "mastas" – mad people, but mad in the love of the beyond. They are mad! For all practical purposes they are mad. They need someone who knows to hold their hand and take them to the fourth. At the third layer a guide who knows, who has passed through the terrain, is needed. And only people of the third layer start searching, hunting for a master, a guide, somebody who can give them help in their moments of chaos.

In the third layer the possibilities are two. You can become mad – that is the fear, that is why people cling to the second layer. They cling, deeply afraid, because if they lose their grip they will be falling into chaos – you all know it, that if you don't cling to the roles you will fall into chaos. You play the game of the husband or the wife – if you drop playing the game you know you will go mad. You go on playing the game that society has enforced on you, afraid that if you drop out of it . . . where will you drop? Drop out of the society and you drop into chaos. Then all certainty is lost, there is only confusion.

So one possibility is confusion, neurosis, the madhouse. Another possibility is, if you remain alert, meditative, aware, the chaos becomes utterly beautiful. Then it is not chaos, it has an order of its own, an inner order of its own. Even the storm is beautiful if you can remain alert in it and don't get identified. Then the chaos surrounds you like a tremendous energy moving all around, and you stand just in the centre, unaffected. Your awareness not touched at all. This gives you for the first time a glimpse of what sanity is.

People who belong to the second layer only look sane, they are not. Force them to the third layer and they will become insane. People who are in the third layer and aware – they are sane and they cannot be forced to become mad. No situation can force them to become mad. People in the second layer are always on the very boundary. A little push – the market goes down, or they go bankrupt, or the wife dies, or the son becomes a criminal – and they fall into the third; they become mad.

People on the second level are always ready to become mad; any situation, just a little push . . . They are cooking at 99 degrees centigrade; only one degree more is needed, and that can happen any moment. They will go mad.

One who moves into the third layer and remains aware goes beyond madness. Then, there is the fourth layer. If you pass through the third, only then can you enter the fourth. If you have faced chaos, if you have faced the anarchy of the inner world, then you become capable of entering the fourth.

The fourth is the layer of death, the death plane. After the chaos one has to face death – the chaos prepares you. On the fourth, if you reach, you will have a sudden feeling of dying – you *are* dying. In deep meditation when you touch the fourth layer you start feeling that you are dying. Or – because meditation is not such a universal experience – in deep sexual orgasm also you can feel that you are dying. All over the world, people of different cultures, language, conditioning, whenever they feel orgasm suddenly a feeling of death overtakes them. People have even been found to utter – particularly women, when they are in deep orgasm and their whole body is vibrating with an unknown rhythm, is filled with vital energy, has become a dance – women all over the world have been known to utter words like: "I am dying! Kill me completely!"

In ancient Indian treatises on sex it is said, "Never keep a parrot or a mynah bird in the love chamber." Because he can learn, when you are making love and you utter such cries of utter joy as "I am dying!" the parrot or the mynah can learn it. Then he can repeat it and it can be embarrassing if he repeats it with guests and other people around. So never keep a parrot in the love chamber.

That's why women have been suppressed all over the world, through the centuries, to not utter a single word – in fact they have been conditioned not to have orgasm because it is dangerous; you feel a deathlike freedom. The ego dies; suddenly the whole identity is lost. "You" are no longer there, just life vibrating – life unknown, life unnamed, life which cannot be categorized. Just *life* – you are not there. The wave has disappeared, only the ocean is there. To have a deep orgasm is to have an oceanic feeling of being totally lost. Women have been forced not to be active in lovemaking, because if they are active they are more prone – because they have a subtler and more delicate body – to feel the deathlike phenomenon of orgasm. They have been forced not to utter a single word, not to move; they should remain just lying dead, frozen.

Men have also become aware that if they really move deep into orgasm it gives a very intense experience, tremendously shaking, shocking; it is a death. The man will never be the same again. So men have learned to have a local orgasm, just at the genitals, the whole body is not involved.

For centuries women completely forgot that they could have orgasm. It is only just a few decades ago that the woman has rediscovered her capacity for orgasm. And not just the capacity for orgasm, but a capacity for multiple orgasms. She is more powerful than the man, and she can move more deeply into orgasm than the man. No man can compete with a woman as far as orgasm is concerned, but it has been suppressed and hidden for centuries. It was taught to her that it is only the man who enjoys sex, not the woman; she was taught that it is not womanly to enjoy it.

Why this suppression, and why all over the world has sex itself been suppressed so deeply? Sex is similar to death; that is the reason. All cultures suppress two things, sex and death. And they are so similar that you can almost say they are two aspects of the same coin. They have to be, because it is through sex that life is born; it must be through sex that life disappears again. The original source must be the end of the circle also. Through sex, the wave of life arises – so it must subside into sex again. So sex *is* life and sex *is* death.

The same happens in meditation. You move into such a deep tuning, turning in, that suddenly you pass the third layer of chaos. You are dying! And if you become afraid, then there will be a block. In people who have become afraid of meditation, and then make all sorts of rationalizations not to do it, a block exists. But if you remain alert and allow death, you become deathless. You know death is happening all around, and you are not dying. Dying and yet not dying, dying utterly and yet utterly alive – that is the most beautiful experience a person can have.

At this fourth stage again two possibilities are there – on every layer two possibilities are there. One is, if you really become dead without awareness, then you will exist like a zombie, a robot, dull, absentminded. You can find in many madhouses people belonging to the fourth layer who have lost all life, all vitality. They exist but their existence is more like vegetating. The person has reached to the very end, and suddenly he could not remain alert. Now he has died. One part of the thing has happened, the other has not happened; he has died and he has not been reborn. The person will remain absent, he will look at you with empty eyes. If you give him food he will eat, if you don't give him food he will sit without eating for days. He will live a dead life. He is at the fourth stage, but he missed awareness.

At the fourth layer, without a master it is almost impossible. Dying is easy on your part, but who will give you rebirth? Who will pull you out of that death experience that is so shocking and shattering that the ego simply drops? The fourth is the experience where the Christian symbol of the cross becomes meaningful. It is at the fourth that the cross is meaningful – one dies, but that is not the whole thing. Jesus resurrects; the cross and resurrection.

If one simply dies at the fourth, one will live the life of a zombie. The person will move in the world as if fast asleep, as if in a deep, hypnotic sleep. Drunk, empty . . . the cross will be there within the person but the resurrection has not happened. If one remains alert . . . and it is very difficult to be alert when death is happening . . . but when one is working slowly, it is possible. If you can become mindful, aware, while death is happening all around, you become deathless. Then comes the fifth layer.

The fifth is the layer of life. Energy becomes absolutely free, with no blocks. You are free to be whatsoever you want to be. To move, not to move, to act, not to act – whatsoever, you are absolutely free. Energy becomes spontaneous. But, for the last time, there are also two possibilities.

One can become so identified with life energy that one can become an epicurean. That is where Epicurus and Buddha separate. Epicureans, the Charvakas in India, and other hedonists of the world have really penetrated to the fifth core of life, they have come to know what life is – and they have become identified with life. Eat, drink, be merry has become their credo because they don't know anything beyond life.

Life is beyond death. You are even beyond life. You are an ultimate transcendence. So in the fifth layer there is a possibility that if you don't remain alert you will become a victim of hedonism. It is good, you have reached close to home; one step more . . . but then you think the goal is achieved. Epicurus is beautiful. One step more and he would have become a Buddha. Charvakas are beautiful, just one step more and they would have become Christs. Just a step more . . . and at the last moment they got identified with life. And remember, to be identified with death is difficult because who wants to be identified with death? But it is very easy to be identified with life because everybody wants to have eternal life, life and life and life . . .

The person who turns at this moment to become an Epicurus, who becomes identified with life, lives a very orgasmic life. His whole body functions in a tremendously beautiful and graceful way. He enjoys small things – eating, dancing, walking in the breeze, sunning. Small things of life give him tremendous enjoyment. Joy is the word for this person, or you can call it delight. But not bliss; bliss is not for him. He enjoys, but he is not blissful.

What is the difference between joy and bliss? When you enjoy something, your joy depends on that thing, it is objective. You have a beautiful woman to love, and you feel joy. But if the beautiful woman goes away, sadness descends. When the climate is good, vibrating, alive, you have a dance to your feet. But then the climate is dull, cloudy, and all joy disappears. The man of joy will feel sadness also. There will be ups and there will be downs, he will move to the peak and come back to the valley. There will be days and nights – duality will remain.

If one remains alert at the moment when life happens – aware, mindful, conscious – one transcends life also. Then there is bliss. Bliss is joy without any cause, visible or invisible. Bliss is uncaused joy. You are happy whatsoever the case. Now, bliss is your nature – not something that happens to you. It is *you*.

These are the layers, and they happen in this way because when a child is born the child *is life*. Every child is Epicurus, life vibrating, freely moving energy with no blocks. A child is energy, sheer delight in energy, just jumping for no reason and so happy that even if you reach paradise you will not jump like that – and he is jumping for nothing! Or he has gathered a few coloured stones and he is simply mad with delight. Watch little children just sitting, doing nothing – and they seem so happy, for no reason at all!

When a child is born he has only one layer, and that is life. If a child can become aware he can move immediately to the state of a buddha – but that is difficult. He cannot become aware because to become aware he will have to move into life, into suffering. He will have to collect many layers; that is part of growth. That's why Jesus says you will enter into the Kingdom of God only when you are like children . . . but he doesn't say that *children* will enter, no. People who are *like* children, not children. Children won't enter; they have to grow, they have to lose all in order to regain it again. They have to be lost in the world, they have to forget themselves completely; only through that going away, far away from themselves, suffering much, will they come back to their home. They will rediscover it – then they are like children. Not children, but *like* children.

A child is born with the life layer functioning. A child has only two layers: the life layer and the transcendental layer. The transcendental is the centre, it is not a layer but the very core. You can call it the soul, the self, or whatever you want to call it. A child has only the one layer of life, and then by and by as the child grows he becomes aware of death. He sees people dying, flowers falling; he sees suddenly a dead bird, or the family dog dies – he becomes aware of death. When he sees things and looks around he starts feeling that life has to end someday. He is accumulating another layer and that is the layer of death; he becomes afraid of death. It is the second layer that a child attains to.

Then, as he grows, there are many shoulds and should-nots: "You should do this and you should not do that." He is not allowed total, chaotic freedom; he is disciplined, forced. The child is a chaos, total freedom; he would like to have no rules in the world, but that cannot be allowed. He is becoming a member of the society, so his chaos, his quick, multi-dimensional energy, has to be suppressed. Rules have to be forced on him, he has to be taught things – there is toilet training and other things, and everything becomes "good" or "bad", divided. He has to choose. A third layer of chaos, or neurosis, is created.

Children who have been taught too many rules carry more neurosis within them; that's why neurosis happens only in a very civilized society. In a primitive society people don't go neurotic; rules were never forced too much on them, in fact they have been allowed to keep their chaos in themselves, a little. Few rules, then few possibilities of neurosis; more rules, more possibilities of neurosis – this is the third layer.

Then the child starts learning how to play games. He has to play games because he is not allowed to be authentic and real. There are times when he feels that he hates his mother, because his mother goes on forcing things on him. But he cannot say this to the mother, that he hates her. He has to say, "I love you." He has to please her, and to pretend that he loves her deeply. Now the games are starting – a fourth layer; he will be playing roles. Small children become politicians. The father comes home and the child smiles, because he knows if you don't smile then you cannot get ice cream today. If you smile, the father becomes generous; his hand goes into his pocket. If you don't smile, he can be very harsh. Now the child has become a politician.

You see pictures of politicians – they are always smiling. Have you seen somebody campaigning for election? He goes on smiling, just stretching the lips – there is no smile inside. Sometimes it happens that it becomes such a habit. I have known one politician: unfortunately one night I had to sleep in the same hotel room with him – in the night I got up and looked and he was smiling! It had become such a habit that even in sleep he could not relax. He must have been campaigning in his dreams or something . . .

The child learns that he has to pretend. He is not accepted as he is; he has to show that he is just as you would like him to be. He becomes divided: now he has a private world of his own. If he wants to smoke a cigarette he has to hide somewhere – he smokes in the garage, or goes outside into some back street to hide himself. You may have seen a child smoking, but ask him and he simply denies it – and so innocently; he says, "What are you saying? Me? Smoking? Never!" And look at his innocent, beautiful face . . . he has become a perfect politician, a role-player.

Then he learns that his games pay. If you are honest, you suffer. If you become expert in lies, it is rewarded. Now the child is learning the ways of the mad world. A fourth layer emerges, of role playing.

Then a fifth layer – that of formalities. Somebody is coming to visit and he hates the person, but the family says, "She is a guest and you have to welcome her; not only welcome her but you have to give her a kiss." The child hates the very idea, it is disgusting! But what to do? A child is helpless, powerless. You have power, the family has power, and you can crush him. So he smiles, and kisses, and says "Good morning" without meaning any of it. Now he is creating a fifth layer.

These are the five layers. You have to go backwards, to the original source. That's what Patanjali calls *pratyahara*, coming back to the original state. That's what Mahavir has called *pratikramana*, coming back, falling back to your originality. That's what Christ has called *conversion*, becoming again a child.

Then, when all layers of your onion are peeled off – it is an arduous thing; even to peel an ordinary onion is difficult, tears will come to your eyes, and when you peel the onion of your own personality there will be many tears. It is hard, it is

42

arduous, but it has to be done; otherwise you live a false life, and you live a sick life.

But a child is ignorant – he does not know, but neither does he know that he does not know. A sage also does not know, but he knows that he does not know – that is the only difference between a child and a sage. The child is ignorant but not aware that he is ignorant; a sage is also ignorant, but perfectly aware that he is ignorant. This is his wisdom, this is his knowing – knowing that he does not know.

To be in between, and to pretend, is to be sick. To pretend is to be false. To be false is to be stuck somewhere. To be stuck somewhere is to be blocked – energy is not flowing, it is not free to move; you are not like a river, but frozen, blocks of ice, part dead and part alive.

Just analyse your own self. What do you know? If you penetrate deeply you will come to understand that you don't know anything. Information you may have much of, but that is not knowing. Scriptures – you may have read many, but that is not knowing. Unless you read the scripture of your own being there is no knowing possible. There is only one Koran and one Bible and one Gita, and that is hidden within you. You have to decode it – and that is what I have been talking to you about, how to decode it, how it has been lost in the jungle of your personalities, layers of personalities, masks, pretensions. It is lost, but it is not lost absolutely, it is still there. Search and it can be found. Seek a little, move toward it, and sooner or later you are on the track. The moment you are on the track you suddenly feel everything falling into place, everything coming together, everything becoming a symphony. The divisions are dissolving and unity is arising.

And knowing is possible only when you transcend life and death, not before. How can you know if you have not even attained to your innermost being? What else can you know if you don't know yourself? Hence the insistence of all sages on "knowing thyself", because that is the secret key of all knowledge. That one key opens a thousand and one locks, it is a master key. Knowing one, say the Upanishads, one knows all. Without knowing that one, even if you know all, it is of no use. It may burden you, it may become heavy on you. It may kill you but it cannot free you.

If you remain alert, and you know a particular block – "Here is where my wound is, here is the impasse, here is the block, the sickness" – if you can be alert to your sickness, suddenly it starts melting.

But this recognition of your sickness, this alertness, is possible only in very deep consciousness, awareness. Recognition means you are alert and you recognize that *this* is the problem. Once you pinpoint the problem, the problem is already on the way to being solved; nothing else is needed. For spiritual disease, recognition alone is enough; no other medicine is needed.

Medicine and meditation – these are the two medicines in the world. And both words come from the same root. Medicine for the body, meditation for the soul, and both mean "medicine".

The sage has no spiritual disease because he is simply alert, watchful. He remembers himself. He is not identified at any layer of the personality. He is not the formalities, he is not the role and playing, he is not the chaos, he is not the death, he is not the life. He is the very transcendence of all.

Take it as a very useful tool; use it in the inner rediscovery of your being. Move from the first layer . . . and don't be in a hurry, because if you leave something incomplete in any layer, you will have to come back to the whole layer. Always remember that anything incomplete will remain a hangover. So when you are searching in one layer, search it *totally*. Be finished with it, don't carry it into another layer. It can be solved only in its own space.

When you enter the second layer of game playing – watch these games, don't be in a hurry. And don't just accept what I am saying, because that won't help. You can say, "Yes, this is what Osho says, and I have come to recognize it." No, that won't help. My recognition can't be your recognition; you have to travel the path on your own feet. I cannot travel for you, at the most I can indicate the way. But you have to follow it, walk, you have to move on it and move very carefully so nothing is left incomplete and unlived. Otherwise that will cling to you, and you will carry it into another layer and everything will be a chaos and confusion.

Be finished with every layer, and when I say be finished, don't misunderstand me – I am not saying stop using that layer, I am not saying stop saying "Good morning" to people – I am saying don't make that your whole world. Say good morning, and if you can mean it, it is beautiful – *mean* good morning! If you are really alive, your formality will also become alive. When you are going to say good morning in any case, why not mean it? When you are already going to say it, because it has to be said, then mean it!

I am not saying drop out of formalities, no, because many times this has been done in the past – people have become fed up with the false pretensions and they drop out of the society. That is a reaction, not a revolution. Then they move to the opposite extreme. Then they don't believe in any formalities and their life becomes difficult and they make others' lives also difficult. They lose smoothness, and they drop all that lubricates.

Enlightenment is Your Nature

For example you can approach a woman, even if she is a stranger, and just ask her: "Would you like to sleep with me?" It may be sincere, you may actually want to do it, but it is aggressive and violent. Even if the woman is ready to go with you, the way you propose it is going to become an obstacle – it hurts; the woman feels as if you are only going to use her. No, a little lubrication is necessary. Or, you go to your father and you simply ask for money, not even saying a good morning first; then it seems that your only relationship is through the money. Things become hard-edged. Things are already hard and without feeling – why make them harder?

So I am not telling you to drop all formalities. They are beautiful – as far as they go, they go beautifully. Just remember one thing: that you should not become the world of the formal. You should remain alert. If somebody is willing, you should be capable of moving to the second layer of game playing. And if somebody is willing you should be able to move to the third layer of chaos. When you love a person, and a person loves you, you can sit together in deep chaos; it has a tremendous, austere beauty to it. Two persons in deep chaos, like two clouds meeting each other. But if somebody is willing, and somebody is ready to move in your chaos – only then, otherwise don't trespass on anybody. Don't interfere with anybody's life – those formalities are just good ways to avoid trespass.

Games and role playing are good, because if somebody is not ready to move deep, who are you to force the person to move deep? There is no point – move yourself! And if somebody is willing to move with you to the fourth, the death level – if somebody is really in love with you and wants an utterly intimate relationship – only then drop the third, move to the fourth, move to the fifth.

From fifth to sixth, the transcendental, you have to move alone. Up to the fifth a master can be helpful. From the fifth to the sixth you have to move alone – but then you are ready; by the time you reach the fifth you are ready. Only one step more, in total aloneness, you dissolve into your own infinity, the inner emptiness.

This is what we have called *nirvana* – the complete cessation of your individual being, as if a drop has fallen into the ocean and has become the ocean. The wave disappears, individuality is no more; you have become the whole. And when you have become the whole, only then, you are really healthy. That is why the sage is not sickminded. In fact, the sage has no mind – how can he be sickminded?

If you ask me, I would like to say that all minds are sick, more or less. To be in the mind is to be sick; degrees differ.

Up to the fifth, there is a possibility of the mind because there is a possibility of getting identified. To get identified with anything is to create a mind. If you get identified with life you create a mind immediately. Mind is nothing but identification. If you remain unidentified, aloof, a watcher on the hill, a witness – then you don't have any mind. Witnessing is not a mental process. All else is mental. So the sage is healthy because he has no mind.

Attain to no-mindness. Move layer by layer, peel your onion completely, until only emptiness is left in your hand.

I am afraid – afraid of enlightenment. What is beyond enlightenment? What to do after the goal of living is reached? What do you aim for? It is like falling into a bottomless pit. You fall – no bottom, no goal. Then what do you aim for? What is beyond the goal?

You have raised very significant questions. I am saying questions because there are many. You have condensed them into a very small question.

First you are saying, "I am afraid, afraid of enlightenment." This can be taken as a general state of human mind; otherwise there is no reason why so few people have ever become enlightened. And those who have become enlightened have been shouting for centuries of its joy, its bliss; its ultimate truth, beauty; its eternity and its going beyond death. But the larger part of humanity has not paid any attention to it, naturally. Your question comes from the deepest core of humanity.

It is not only your question; everybody is afraid of enlightenment. And the reason is clear why one is afraid: the fear is of losing yourself. For the same reason people are afraid of love; for the same reason people are afraid of trust; for the same reason they remain enclosed in all kinds of fears, miseries, anxieties and anguish, because at least these feel familiar. And one thing is certain, they don't ask you to be lost. The more painful your life is, the more you are.

Perhaps deep down you desire pain, you desire misery, you desire anguish, because that keeps you clearly defined. You are afraid of the same things for which you also have a longing. On the one hand, there is a longing to go beyond all fears, beyond all anxieties, beyond all suffering. But the problem becomes complex, because being beyond suffering you are also beyond yourself – you are the suffering. You are the prison, that's why you are afraid to get out of it. On the contrary, you try to console yourself in every way, that "This is not a prison, this is my home."

So you are living in a dilemma: you want to go into the open sky and open your wings and fly across the sun. But

48

on the other hand, you are afraid you may never be able to find the way back to your cosy, familiar space. Although it is painful you have become accustomed to it; although there is suffering it is like an old friend. The beyond invites you, calls you to take courage. But it also creates a trembling within you, because going out of the cosy circle of your misery and your hell, you know for certain – you may not be very conscious of it – that your so-called personality will melt away into the vast ocean, just like an ice block.

The fear is, is there something beyond your personality? You are not aware of it, you have never come across it – you have never met yourself. You know only the superficial that has been told to you. You don't know on your own authority your essential, your inner. And of course nobody else can say anything about your inner. It is not available for observation; it is not available to be an object. Science cannot find it. Logic feels absolutely inadequate. Reason has not the wings to fly to the inner.

Karl Marx used to say, "I will believe in God only if he is caught in a test tube and scientists unanimously declare that this is God – after dissection and autopsy to find whether he is really divine." Karl Marx was representative of you all, of the wider humanity; he is saying, "How can I believe in God? Science has no proof for it." And science has no proof either for your self. It can dissect you, it can cut you into as many parts as possible, but it will not find you; it will find only a dead corpse.

Only very recently have geniuses become aware that what we have been doing in physiology, in biology, in medical sciences, is not right. The moment you take blood out of my body and then you test it, it is not the same blood that is flowing in my body. In my body it is alive, it has a life of

49

its own; outside my body it is a dead thing. And you cannot conclude from the analysis of the dead about the living. You can take anything out of the human body, but the moment you take it out, you have taken it out as a dead thing. In the human body it was an organic, living, breathing, alive part.

A few very sensitive medical surgeons have become aware of the fact that something has to be done about it, because in the medical colleges they go on studying the corpses, skeletons, to decide about living human beings – there is such a great logical fallacy. But they are also feeling impotent – how to approach life? All that they know is – their whole technology, their whole methodology is to know – the object, and you are not the object. Hence, science is never going to accept your living being – it is beyond its limits. Logic cannot accept, reason cannot accept, philosophy cannot accept.

And your fear, on top of it all, is that nobody is there to give you a certainty that beyond your superficial personality there is something more. You will disappear as you are, and you will appear in your authentic reality. This is the fear. People are afraid of coming closer to each other, even in love; they keep each other at arm's length. They want to come closer, but a fear . . . to be too close, you can be lost.

With love, the problem is not so great – but going beyond your ordinary self, your accepted face that you have seen in the mirror, that others have told you is very beautiful, or is ugly . . . All your knowledge about yourself is dependent on others' opinions.

This is your personality – this is not your individuality. You cannot do such a thing with an individual who has a groundedness. The fear is because you don't have any experience of your innermost being; all that you know about yourself is what people have said. And these are the people who don't know anything about themselves – what can they know about you?

Everybody is afraid of enlightenment, because who knows? Once your personality disappears maybe everything disappears. Then what is the point of such an enlightenment? It is better to remain unenlightened – at least you *are*. And death may come whenever it may come, but right now you are alive – why unnecessarily commit a suicide?

Enlightenment appears to your personality as a suicide, and in fact it is a suicide. But the suicide of personality is the beginning of individuality. The death of your personality and ego is the birth of your real authentic being, of your immortality. You will have to gather courage, and remember Michel's Rule for Prospective Mountain Climbers: the mountain gets steeper as you get closer to the top.

So as you come closer to enlightenment – and that is the greatest mountain – it gets steeper, and more and more dangerous as you come close to the disappearance of your old personality with which you were so identified.

But I tell you, I have survived. I have lost my personality; that's why I am not at all concerned what people think about me. The whole world is against me, but they don't even create a small stir in me. It does not matter whether they are against or for; it is their business, their problem. I know myself, and I know that what I am doing and what I am trying is intrinsically right. Nobody, just because they are in the majority, can destroy my truth.

Truth has never been the opinion of the majority; it has always been an individual achievement. The majority is interested in crucifying the truth, but it is not ready to accept it.

You can understand the psychology of it all. For two thousand years Christians have been thinking about Jesus and his crucifixion. And I am utterly disappointed with the whole two thousand years' theology, because they have not looked at the psychology of the crucifixion. Why did people crucify Jesus? He had not done any wrong; he has not committed any crime. But the majority was turning against him because he was telling them, "Drop your ego; be humble. Drop your so-called false identity; just be nobody. Blessed are those who stand last in the line."

He was talking against the ambitious majority. They did not crucify Jesus, they crucified the truth that was hurting them and was making them afraid: if they become impressed by this man, there is a danger. They may lose half the bread in the hope of the whole bread, and there may not be any bread at all. It is better to keep the half and not to lose it in the hope of getting the whole. That is the majority's mind.

You say, "I am afraid – afraid of enlightenment." It is natural, so don't be serious about it. In a way, it is a good symptom – at least you have become interested in enlightenment; otherwise, you would not be afraid. Just go into the town and you will not find anybody . . . ask people, "Are you afraid of enlightenment?" And they will say, "Why should we be afraid?" They have never bothered about it. It is not a problem to them, they have never thought about enlightenment. They will think you are crazy. "Why should we be afraid of enlightenment?"

Just the other day I was looking at a newspaper clipping. It was a statement against me, that the world is coming to an end but I seem to be the only person who is not going to change, who is still talking about enlightenment. As far as I am concerned, I take it as a compliment. When the world is coming to an end, this is the right moment.

Take the risk; anyway it is going to end.

Why not take a chance and become enlightened?

The world is coming to an end – you will end with it. So now there is no fear: before the world ends, end your personality, and at least you will be saved. The world may end, but you will not end. And the person who has criticized me is right. I will go on insisting. My insistence will become more and more powerful as the end of the world comes near, to make more and more people interested in enlightenment because there is no problem about losing; you can put the fear aside.

The fear is a good symptom – it means you have become interested in enlightenment and your mind is trembling. You have become interested in the great adventure, the great affair, and your small personality is worried that this is the end. As for the small personality, which consists only of public opinions, it is going to dissolve – naturally.

It is said that every river before entering the ocean stops for a while and looks back – a moment of hesitation about what she is going to do. Ahead is the vast ocean, in which she is going to be lost. Back, she had a personality of her own – her own mountains, valleys, forests. The whole journey, long journey, maybe thousands of years, thousands of miles . . . Naturally, it is understandable to hesitate for a moment. But I have never seen any river go backwards. You can hesitate, but you cannot go backwards. You have to take the jump. Only by taking the jump will you prove your mettle.

"What is beyond enlightenment?" First things first! Out of fear you are thinking that it seems enlightenment is bound to happen; now be clear what is going to happen after it – "What is beyond enlightenment?"

Beyond enlightenment is all – the whole universe. Beyond enlightenment you are no more a small dewdrop, you are the ocean.

"What to do after the goal of living is reached?" You are not supposed to do anything. I can see all your concerns are very human. You know one thing, that now you cannot avoid enlightenment; you may be afraid, but you have to take the jump. Naturally, you are asking, "What is beyond enlightenment?" And even if something is there – "What to do after the goal of living is reached?"

You have never thought about what you have done as far as your birth is concerned – have you done anything? What are you doing as far as your life is concerned? Do you think you are breathing? If it was up to you to breathe, you would have been dead long before; just in anger, or in some love affair, you would forget to breathe. Or in the night, will you sleep or not? Or keep yourself awake just to continue breathing, because if you fall asleep and breathing stops, in the morning who is going to get up? No, breathing you are not doing.

Existence is breathing.

What are you doing as far as your inner structure of life is concerned? Do you digest? Are you responsible for changing food into blood, into bones, into marrow? These are not your concerns. Your concern ends with the taste buds, and the moment the food is swallowed it goes into the hands of existence; it is no more your concern.

One day try to be continuously aware what is happening in your stomach, and then you will have a good disturbed stomach for at least one week! Your consciousness is not needed, the stomach is doing its work on its own. Your brain consists of billions of cells, and each cell is doing its own function, and you are not needed – they don't even ask your advice. Has any part of your body stopped you sometime and asked you, "What to do? – I am at a loss?" They are never at a loss; they are part of the cosmic organism. They have an inbuilt process; they go on doing their things.

The moment you become enlightened and disappear into the ocean, you will not be asked to do something – to type, or to dig, or to prepare pizza! You are not supposed to do anything; you are gone. Now the universal force has taken possession of you. Things will be happening, but they will not be your doing.

"What do you aim for?" You have reached beyond aim. Aim is a concern of the ego. The ego cannot exist without an aim – some ambition, some desire, some infatuation, something to be achieved tomorrow.

The ego is a tension between today and the future. The moment there is no ego, there is no tension. You simply live in a state of let-go.

Then, wherever the river takes you, wherever the life force takes you, you simply go. It is not your goal; you have become part of the whole. Now whatever is the goal of the whole . . . And I don't think there is any goal – the whole is perfectly happy in singing and dancing and enjoying; in flowers, in the wind, in the rain, in the sun, in the stars, there is no goal. The whole is perfectly happy just to be, here-now.

If there is no aim, you start thinking it is like falling into a bottomless pit. Then what to do and what to aim for? "What is beyond the goal?" You are really in trouble! You will not be satisfied unless you are enlightened. All these problems: first, "What is the goal?" Then, "What is beyond the goal?" You want to determine the whole eternity!

Your question should be just about enlightenment. Beyond that, existence takes care.

Use your intelligence to see that the fear is arising out of the false in you, the fear is not arising out of the real. The real is really deeply challenged by the idea of enlightenment. But be intelligent; otherwise you may listen to the personality and forget to listen to the individuality.

Meditate more, so that your intelligence can become more clear, unclouded, and all fears will disappear. And all other questions are just nonsense; they will also disappear. All that you need is a little more meditation, a little more sharpness of intelligence.

Paddy and Maureen planned to get married, so they went to the doctor for a physical check-up. The doctor then tried to explain sex to them, but Paddy just listened with a dumb expression on his face. So the doctor took Maureen over to the examination table, made her lie down, and then made love to her. "Now do you understand?" said the physician.

"Yes," said Paddy, "but how often do I have to bring her in?"

A great question! Just become enlightened. Don't get worried about so many problems. You will be lost in a jungle of a thousand and one problems. And enlightenment is a simple process; it is just becoming your authentic self. And it is so luminous that in its light all darkness disappears, and with the darkness all the doubts, all the questions. And a tremendous insight arises that you are not separate from existence; hence there is no question of goal, no question of direction; no question where you are going, why you are going.

Then, just to be part of the whole is so immense and so overwhelming, one feels fulfilled and contented. There is nowhere to go; you have arrived.

The theatrical agent, trying to sell a new strip act to a nightclub manager, was carrying on very excitedly about a girl's unbelievable 72, 26, 40 figure.

"What kind of dance does she do?" the manager enquired, impressed by the description of the girl's figure.

"Well, she doesn't actually dance at all," the agent replied. "She just crawls out onto the stage and tries to stand up!"

With that kind of figure . . . how can you dance?

You have come to the right place. Here we are not giving you any goals, any heaven, any paradise. We are not selling any future to you. We are not in any business – the churches are, the temples are, the synagogues are. I am teaching you that there is no goal and that there is no meaning, but there is great joy, and great love and great blissfulness. And all that you have to pay for it is to drop your false ego, your false personality.

Become silent. In your silence, all questions will disappear. And the dance will begin, whatever the figure! Because as far as your inner being is concerned, it has no figure; it is just a luminous flame which can dance. It has been eternally there, repressed by you. You are the greatest enemy of yourself. My effort is to turn you into the greatest friend of yourself.

Inside and Outside
the Box

Western psychology studies the mind as an object, from the outside. Of course, it misses much. In fact, the most essential is missed. Only the periphery can be understood that way. The innermost is not objective, the innermost is subjective. You can study it from the within, not from the without.

It is as if somebody wants to study love and watches two lovers hugging each other, holding hands, sitting together, making love – goes on collecting data about how two lovers behave. This won't give him any idea of what love is, because love is not on the surface. The surface can be very deceiving, the appearance can be very deceiving. Love is something very inner. Only by being in love do you know it – there is no other way to know it.

Western psychology tries to understand mind from the outside. The very approach makes mind material. Only matter can be understood from the outside, because matter has no inside to it. The mind can only be understood from the inside, because mind has no outside to it – that's the first thing. That's why psychology goes on becoming more and more behavioristic, more and more materialistic, more and more mechanical – and more and more suspicious about the soul of man. The soul is completely denied by Western psychology. Not that the soul does not exist, but because the very approach prohibits it, the very approach becomes a limitation. The conclusion depends on the approach. If you start wrongly, you end wrongly.

The second thing to be understood is that Western psychology tries to understand mind, not to go beyond it – because psychologists think there is no beyond to the mind, it is the end. In the Eastern approach, the mystic also tries to understand mind – not in order to understand mind itself, but to go beyond it. The understanding is to be used as a stepping-stone.

So the mystic is not concerned with the details of the mind. An essential understanding of the functioning of the mind will do. If you go into details there is no end to it. The Eastern approach also studies dreams, but just to make you awake, that's all. Dreaming itself is not the concern. It does not go deep into the dreaming structure, and it does not go on ad infinitum analysing dreams. It simply tries to find the essential structure of the dream in order to transcend it, so you can become a witness. It is totally different.

For example, if I give you a seed of a beautiful tree, and you become too concerned with the seed and you try to understand it, and you dissect it, and you go on and on trying to understand and dissect, and dissect more – the chemical structure, the physical structure, the atomic structure, the electrons, the neutrons – and you go on and on, you completely forget that the seed was meant only to become a tree.

And however deep your dissection, by dissecting a seed you are never going to come to the tree. You will come to the atomic structure of the seed; you will come to the chemical structure of the seed; you may come to the electrical structure of the seed, but that has nothing to do with the tree. And the more you dissect the seed, the further away you are from the tree. Your dissection is not going to bloom. Your dissection is not going to spread its fragrance. And one day, if you have dissected it too much and then you put it in the soil, it won't sprout. It is already dead! In your dissection you killed it, you murdered it.

The Western psychologist is interested in mind just like this example of you being too much obsessed with the seed. The Eastern approach to consciousness is also interested in the seed, but not for its own sake – it is interested in the seed because it carries a potentiality, a possibility of becoming a beautiful tree, a possibility of blossoms, a possibility of fragrance, a possibility of song and dance, a possibility that many birds can come and make their nests on it and many travellers can rest under its shade. But the concern is not the seed – the concern is the tree.

I hope you can see the difference. The concern of the buddhas about the mind is only as a stepping-stone. The mind has to be understood because we are entangled in it.

Let us take another example.

You are thrown in a jail, in a prison cell. One person tries to understand the structure of the jail only to find out ways how to escape from it. Is there a gutter that can be used to escape? Is there a stupid guard who can be fooled? Is there a window that can be broken? Is there a wall you can climb over? Is there a right moment, when guards change and a gap exists? Is there a time in the night when guards fall asleep? Or, are there other prisoners who are also interested in getting out of the prison, so you can be together and help each other? – because climbing the wall alone may be difficult, getting out of the prison alone may be difficult. A group can be created and the group can become a power. You try to understand the structure of the jail just to get out of it.

But if you get too interested in all these details and you completely forget the goal, and you go on studying the jail – the walls and the warden and the prisoners and the guards, and you go on making maps about the structure – then it is stupid. Modern psychology is a little stupid.

In the East we had also developed a tremendously significant psychology. I call it the psychology of the buddhas. But their whole interest was in how to get out of the prison of the mind, how to use its structure to go beyond it. Modern psychology is absolutely obsessed with the structure of the mind and has completely forgotten the goal.

These two differences are vital. The psychology of the buddhas, a psychology based in meditation, understands from within. Of course, then it is a totally different thing. When you study mind from the outside, you study somebody else's mind; it is never yours. And if you go to the labs of psychologists you will be surprised: they go on studying the minds of rats to understand the human mind. It is humiliating, it is very disrespectful. The understanding that is based on the rat's mind cannot be of much help.

But when a meditator watches his own mind, he watches the human mind alive, throbbing, beating. He watches his own mind because that is the closest you can get to the mind. From the outside you can never get very close to the mind; from the outside you can infer, but it will remain inference. It can never become knowledge, because even rats can deceive you, and they have been found to do just that! Even rats are not just on the surface; their innermost core remains inaccessible.

Why do psychologists go on studying rats? Why not man directly? Because man seems to be too complex, so they study elementary structures. It is as if you want to study Einstein and you go to a primary school and you study a small child;

and from that understanding you develop the understanding of an Einstein. It is simply absurd. It is not right at all, the direction is wrong. Every child is not going to become an Einstein. If psychologists were right, then every child would develop into an Einstein. But every child is not going to become an Einstein. Only a certain child has flowered as Einstein. If you want to understand Einstein, the only way is to understand Einstein.

But how to understand an Einstein? From the outside he is as ordinary as anybody else. His distinction is inner, his uniqueness is inner. If you study his blood, his blood is just like anybody else's. If you study his bones, they are just like anybody else's. In fact, Einstein's brain was studied after his death – nothing special. That is something to be noted. Nothing special has been found, but certainly he was a unique man, you cannot deny it. Maybe there has never before existed such a subtle mind on the earth. Nobody ever had such glimpses as he had, but the brain seems to be as ordinary as anybody else's.

The brain is not the mind. It is as if one day I am gone and you go into my room and you study the room, and you try to find out what type, what manner of man this was who lived in this room.

The mind is the guest, the brain is the host. When the mind is gone, the brain is left. The brain is just the room you used to live in. If you study the mind from the outside you can dissect, but you will find only the brain, not the mind. And to study the brain is not to study the mind.

Mind is elusive, you cannot hold it in your hand. You cannot force it into a test tube. The only way to know it is to know it from within, from your witnessing self. The more you become aware, the more you can watch your mind – its subtle functioning. The functioning is tremendously complex and beautiful. Mind is the most complex phenomenon on the earth, the most subtle flowering of consciousness. If you want to really understand what the mind is, then you will have to detach yourself from your mind, and you will have to learn how to be just a witness. That's what meditation is all about.

You have spoken about non-identification, that one should become a witness. But many people are alienated, they cannot get involved, they are simply indifferent to everything. Please can you make clear the difference between non-identification and alienation?

The difference is very clear, but subtle and delicate. To be indifferent means to be dead; it does not mean that you are a witness, it simply means you are disconnected from life and all the sources that nourish you. You are only uprooted; that is alienation.

Uproot a tree and it will start dying. Its greenness will be gone, soon the foliage will wither away, flowers will not come any more. The spring will come and go but the tree will know nothing of it; it has become alienated from existence. It is no longer rooted in the earth, it is no longer related to the sun, it no longer has any bridge. It is surrounded by walls, all bridges are broken.

That's what has happened to the modern man: he is an uprooted tree. He has forgotten how to relate with existence, he has forgotten how to whisper with the clouds and the trees and the mountains. He has completely forgotten the language of silence . . . because it is the language of silence that becomes a bridge between you and the universe that surrounds you. The universe knows no other language. On the earth there are three thousand languages; existence knows no language except the language of silence.

> An English general was talking to a German general after the Second World War. The German was very puzzled; he said, "We had the best equipped army in the world, the best war technology, the greatest leader that history has ever known, the best of generals, and such a devoted army. Why? – why couldn't we win? It seems simply impossible that we have been defeated! It is unbelievable – although it has happened – but we cannot believe it!"
>
> The English general laughed and said, "There is one thing you have forgotten: before starting any battle we used to pray to God; that is the secret of our victory."
>
> The German said, "But we also used to pray to God, every morning!"
>
> The English general laughed and he said, "We know that you used to pray, but you pray in German and we pray in English – and who told you that God knows German?"

Everybody thinks his language is the language of God. Hindus say Sanskrit is the holy language, the divine language – *deva vani* – God understands only Sanskrit. And ask the Mohammedans – then God understands only Arabic; otherwise, why should he have revealed the Koran in Arabic? And ask the Jews – then God understands only Hebrew.

God understands no language because "God" means this total existence. Existence understands only silence – and we have forgotten silence.

Because we have forgotten silence, forgotten the art of meditation, we have become alienated. We have become small, dirty, muddy pools and we don't know how to go and be one with the ocean. We go on becoming dirtier every day, shallower every day, because the water goes on evaporating. We are just muddy, our life has no clarity. Our eyes cannot see and our hearts cannot feel.

This state is the state of indifference; it is a negative state. The mystics have called it "the dark night of the soul". It is not witnessing, it is just the opposite of witnessing.

When I say be a witness I am not saying become uprooted from life. I am saying live life in all its multi-dimensionality, and yet remain aware. Drink the juices of life, but remember that while you are drinking the juices of life there is a consciousness in you beyond all action, all doing. Drinking, eating, walking, sleeping, are all acts, and there is a consciousness in you which simply reflects, a mirror-like phenomenon. It is not indifference. The mirror is not indifferent to you, otherwise why should it bother to reflect you at all? It is immensely interested in you, it reflects you, but it does not become attached. The moment you are gone, you are gone; the mirror does not remain remembering you; the mirror now reflects that which is in front of it.

A witnessing consciousness lives in life but with tremendous non-attachment, with great non-possessiveness; it possesses nothing. It lives totally, it lives passionately, but still knowing that "I don't possess anything."

The witnessing consciousness is not an island separate from the ocean; it is one with the ocean. But still a miracle, a paradox: even being one with the ocean there is a part that remains above the ocean like the tip of the iceberg. That part is your witnessing soul. To create it is the greatest treasure in the world; one becomes a buddha by creating it.

Falling into indifference you become simply unconscious, you go into a coma. You lose all joy in life; the celebration of life stops for you. Then you don't exist, you only vegetate. Then you are not a man but only a cabbage – and that too uprooted. You become more and more rotten every day, you stink; no fragrance comes out of you. The same energy that could have become fragrance passing through a witnessing soul becomes a stinking phenomenon by becoming indifferent.

But I can understand your question. From the outside sometimes indifference and witnessing may appear alike. This has been one of the greatest calamities – because they *appear* alike. Hence true *sannyas* was lost, and a phony *sannyas* became predominant. I call *sannyas* phony if it lives in indifference.

The phony *sannyas* is escapist. It teaches you not to enjoy life, it teaches you not to love music, it teaches you not to cherish beauty. It teaches you to destroy all the sources that beautify your existence. It teaches you to escape to the caves, ugly caves, to turn your back toward the world that existence has given as a gift to you.

The phony *sannyas* is escapist; cheap it is, easy it is. It is very easy to escape from the world and live in a cave and feel holy – because there is no opportunity for you to be unholy, no challenge. Nobody insults you, nobody criticizes you. There is nobody present, so you can think that now there is no anger in you, you can feel that now there is no ego in you. Come back to the world! . . .

I know people who have lived for 30 years in the Himalayas, and when they come back to the world they are surprised to find that they are the same people, nothing has changed. Thirty years of Himalayas – a sheer wastage! But while they were in the Himalayas they were thinking they had become very sacred, very holy, they had become great saints. And there were reasons for them to think so, because no anger, no ego, no greed . . . there is nothing to possess so you feel non-possessive, nobody to compete with so you feel non-competitive, nobody hurts your ego so you don't feel the ego at all.

Things are felt only when there is some hurt. For example, you feel your head only when there is a headache. When the headache disappears, the head also disappears from your consciousness; you cannot feel your head without a headache. You become headless when there is no headache.

Living in the Himalayan cave you have escaped from all the hurts of the world which make you aware again and again of the ego, of the anger, of the greed, of jealousy . . . Coming back into the world you will find everything is back again – and back with a vengeance, because for 30 years it has been accumulating. You will bring a bigger ego than you had ever taken with you to the Himalayas.

The *sannyas* that teaches indifference is phony. The *sannyas* that teaches you how to live in the world and yet float above it like a lotus flower, like a lotus leaf, remaining in the water and yet untouched by the water, remaining in the world and yet not allowing the world to enter into you, being in the world yet not being *of* the world – that is true renunciation.

That true renunciation comes through witnessing; it is not indifference. Indifference will make you alienated, being alienated you will feel meaningless, joyless, accidental. Feeling accidental, the desire to commit suicide will arise, is bound to arise. Why go on living a meaningless life? Why go on repeating the same rut, the same routine, every day? If there is no meaning, why not end it all, why not be finished with it all?

Hence many more people are committing suicide every day, many people are going mad every day. The rate of suicide and madness is increasing. Psychoanalysis seems to be of no help. Psychoanalysts, in fact, commit suicide more, go mad more, than any other profession.

Nothing seems to help the modern man – because the indifference is too heavy; it has created a dark cloud around him. He cannot see beyond his own nose; he is suffocating in his lonely world. The walls are so thick, thicker than the China Wall, that even when you love you are hidden behind your wall, your beloved is hidden behind her wall. There are two China Walls between you. You shout, but no communication seems to be possible. You say one thing, something else is understood; she says something, you understand something else. Husbands and wives sooner or later come to one understanding: that it is better not to talk. It is better to keep silent, because the moment you utter a word, misunderstanding is bound to follow.

All communication has disappeared from the world. Everybody is living a lonely life – lonely in the crowd; the crowd is becoming bigger and bigger every day. The world population is exploding; there have never been so many human beings as there are today – and man has never been so lonely. Strange! Why are we so lonely amid such a crowd? Communication has failed.

Gaffney staggered into a bar crying. "What happened?" asked Brady the bartender.

"I did a horrible thing," sniffed the drunk. "Just a few hours ago I sold my wife to someone for a bottle of Scotch."

"That's awful," said Brady. "Now she is gone and you want her back, right?"

"Right," said Gaffney, still crying.

"You are sorry you sold her because you realized too late that you love her, right?"

"Oh, no," said the Irishman, "I want her back because I am thirsty again!"

It is becoming more and more difficult to understand people, because such thick, dense indifference surrounds everybody that even if you shout you can't be heard, or they hear something which you have not said at all. They hear that which they want to hear or they hear that which they *can* hear. They hear not what is said but what their mind interprets.

Two teenage girls wandered into a photographer's shop in Alabama to have their photos taken.

The photographer sat them down and then busied himself under the black cloth behind his camera.

"What's he doin'?" whispered one girl to her friend.

"He's gonna focus," she whispered back.

"What, both of us?"

D'Angelo, the immigrant, had to travel by train from New York to Raleigh, North Carolina. When he was met by a cousin it was obvious that D'Angelo was in a very bad mood.

"What happened?" asked his relative.

"Ah, that goddamn-a conductor he tell-a me no do this and no do that!" exclaimed the Italian. "I take out-a my sand-a-wich and he say, 'No – inna dining car.' I start-a drink-a some vino and he say, 'No – inna club-a car.' So I go inna club-a car, meet-a girl, and she take-a me back to her empty compartment and then the goddamn conductor he come along ana yell, 'No'foka Virginia, No'foka Virginia!'"

You understand that which you can understand. Your mind is always there to interpret, and the interpretation is yours. It has nothing to do with what you have been told.

People are becoming more and more lonely, and out of desperation they are trying every possible way to communicate. Nothing seems to help. Nothing can help unless they start learning the art of silence. Unless a man and woman know what silence is, unless they can sit together in deep silence, they cannot merge into each other's being. Their bodies may penetrate each other, but their souls will remain far apart. And when souls meet, there is communion, there is understanding.

Indifference makes you dull, makes you mediocre, makes you unintelligent. If you are indifferent your sword will lose all sharpness. That's how it happens to the monks in the monasteries. Look at their faces, in their eyes, and you can see that something is dead. They are like corpses walking, doing things robot-like because those things have to be done. They are not really involved; they have become utterly incapable of getting involved in anything.

This is a very sad situation, and if it continues, man has no future. If it continues, then the third world war is bound to happen – so that we can commit a global suicide; so there is no need to commit suicide retail, we can commit it wholesale. In one single moment the whole earth can die.

Hence meditation has become something absolutely needed, the only hope for humanity to be saved, for the earth to still remain alive. Meditation simply means the capacity to get involved yet remain unattached. It looks paradoxical – all great truths are paradoxical. You have to experience the paradox; that is the only way to understand it. You can do a thing joyously and yet just be a witness that you are doing it, that you are not the doer.

Try with small things, and you will understand. Tomorrow when you go for a morning walk, enjoy the walk – the birds in the trees and the sunrays and the clouds and the wind. Enjoy, and still remember that you are a mirror; you are reflecting the clouds and the trees and the birds and the people.

This self-remembering, Buddha calls *sammasati* – right mindfulness. Krishnamurti calls it "choiceless awareness", the Upanishads call it "witnessing", Gurdjieff calls it "self-remembering", but they all mean the same. But it does not mean that you have to become indifferent; if you become indifferent you lose the opportunity to self-remember.

Go on a morning walk and still remember that you are not it. You are not the walker but the watcher. And slowly you will have the taste of it – it is a taste, it comes slowly. And it is the most delicate phenomenon in the world; you cannot get it in a hurry. Patience is needed.

Eat, taste the food, and still remember that you are the watcher. In the beginning it will create a little trouble in you because you have not done these two things together. In the beginning, I know, if you start watching you will feel like stopping eating, or if you start eating you will forget watching.

Our consciousness is one-way – right now, as it is – it goes only toward the target. But it can become two-way: it can eat and yet watch. You can remain settled in your centre and you can see the storm around you; you can become the centre of the cyclone. And that is the greatest miracle that can happen to a human being, because that brings freedom, liberation, truth, godliness, bliss, benediction.

Waking Up
from the Dream

A man asleep can dream himself anywhere in the universe. From that point, to be awake will look thousands of lives away. But it is a dream; as far as the real sleep is concerned, awakening is just close by.

Any moment you can wake up. Any situation can make you awake. And a master's work is to create devices in which you can become awake. Sometimes very small things – just throwing cold water in your eyes will make you awake. Asleep you were so far away, but when you wake up then you will see that it was a dream that created the distance. Dreaming is the distance. Of course, sleep is necessary for dreaming – but the moment you are awake sleep disappears, and with it the whole world of dreams too.

The truth is that awakening is the nearest reality to you, just by the side of you. It is not far away; hence it cannot be made a goal. All goals are dreaming, all achievements are dreaming. Awakening cannot be a goal because the man who is asleep cannot even think of what awakening can be. He cannot make, in his sleep, a goal of enlightenment – it is impossible. Or whatever he makes will be totally different from the reality of enlightenment.

Enlightenment is part of your waking consciousness.

In the East we talk about four layers of consciousness. First, that one we know is called so-called wakefulness. It is not really wakeful, because just underneath it dreams are floating. Close your eyes and you will have a daydream. Close your eyes and you will immediately see images – imagination takes over, and you start going away from this moment, from here. In reality you are going nowhere, but in your mind you can go anywhere.

So the first state is the so-called waking state; the second state is called sleep. We are aware of these.

The third is called the dreaming state, because sleep can be without dreaming; then it has a different quality. It is very peaceful, very silent, dark and deep . . . very rejuvenating.

So sleep is the second stage, below the so-called waking stage, and then comes the third stage, dreaming. Most of the time in your sleep you are dreaming. If you sleep eight hours, then for six hours you are dreaming. Just here and there, like small islands, you are asleep; otherwise it is continuous dreaming.

You don't remember it, that's why people think this seems too much – six hours of dreaming and only two hours of sleep? You remember only the last dreams when you are waking up, because only with your waking up does your memory start functioning; it catches only the tail-end of your dream world. You don't remember all the dreams, but only the dreams that happen just before you are waking up – the morning dreams.

It was always understood in the East that these six hours of dreaming are as essential as those two hours of silent sleep. But in the West, within the last few years for the first time new research has proved the Eastern insight to be completely right. In fact, the new findings say that dreaming is even *more* essential than sleep, because in dreaming you are throwing out the rubbish of your mind.

73

The whole day the mind is collecting all kinds of words, all kinds of desires, ambitions – too much dust! It has to be thrown out. In the day you don't have any time to throw it out; you are gathering more and more. So in the night when you are asleep the mind has a chance to clean itself up. Dreaming is a kind of spring-cleaning. But it is an everyday business: again you will collect, again you will dream, again you will collect . . .

These are the states known to us. The fourth is not named in the East, but is simply called the fourth, *turiya*. It is a number, it is not a word. No name is given to it so that you cannot interpret it, so that your mind cannot play with it and deceive you. What can the mind do, just listening to the number four? The mind simply feels paralysed. Give any name with meaning, then the mind has a way – meaning is its way. But the number four has no meaning.

The fourth state is the real awakening. The fourth state has to be understood in reference to the other three states. It has something similar to the first, the so-called waking state. The so-called waking state is very thin, almost negligible, but it has some quality of the fourth. The fourth consists *only* of that quality; it is pure awakening. You are fully awake.

It also has some similarity to the second stage, the stage of dreamless sleep. This sleep has silence, depth, peacefulness, relaxation, but in a very small measure – just as much as is needed for day-to-day affairs. But the fourth has its totality – total relaxation, total silence, abysmal depth.

It has also some quality of the dream. The dream takes you far away from yourself. You may go to the moon in the dream, you may go to some star in the dream, although you remain here, in your bed. In reality you don't go anywhere, but in imagination – as long as you are dreaming – it looks absolutely real. You cannot think in a dream that it is a dream. If you can realize in a dream that it is a dream, the dream will be broken – you are awake, and you cannot catch hold of the dream again.

One Sufi story about Mulla Nasruddin is that one night he dreams that an angel is giving him some money, "Because you are so virtuous, so wise, God has sent some reward for you." But as the mind is, when the angel gives him ten rupees, Mulla says, "This is not a reward – don't insult me." And slowly he brings the angel up to 99 rupees. But Mulla is stubborn; he says, "I will take a hundred or I will not take anything. What a miserly approach it is – and from God! You represent God and you cannot make it a hundred?"

He shouted so loudly, "Either a hundred or nothing!" that it woke him up. He looked all around – there was nobody, just he was sleeping in his bed. He said, "My God, I lost 99 rupees unnecessarily, just being stubborn for one rupee more." He closed his eyes, tried hard, "Please come back, wherever you are. Ninety-nine is okay; even 98 will do . . . 97 is also all right – anything will do. You just come back! Where are you?"

He came all the way back down to one rupee, "I will take only one rupee . . . anything from God is great. I was foolish to call God a miser; in fact, I was greedy. Forgive me, and give me just one rupee." But the angel was not there.

You cannot catch hold of the same dream again. And once you are awakened there is no way to catch hold of the same dream.

A dream takes you away from yourself; that's its basic quality. Perhaps that's why it cleanses you and helps you to have a certain relaxation: you forget your worries. For a few moments at least you can be in paradise, you can be in situations you always wanted to be in.

The fourth stage also has something similar, but just similar. It also takes you away from yourself – but forever. You cannot come back to yourself. In the dream you cannot come back to the same dream; in the fourth stage you cannot come back to the same self. It takes you really so far away that you can be the whole universe. That's what the Eastern mystics have said: *Aham Brahmasmi* – I have become the whole.

But you have to lose the self.

You cannot come back to it.

This fourth stage has been given different names. This is the most mathematical name, "the fourth". It was given by Patanjali, who was a very scientific and mathematical mystic. His treatise has remained for thousands of years the only source of yoga. Nothing has been added, because nothing more is needed. It is very rare that one person creates a complete system, so complete and so perfect that it is impossible to change anything in it.

In the West it used to be thought that Aristotle was such a person – he created logic, the whole system of logic alone, and for two thousand years it remained the same. But in the past century things have changed, because new discoveries in physics have made it absolutely necessary to find something better than Aristotle. The new findings in physics have created a problem, because if you follow Aristotle's logic then you cannot accept those findings. Those findings are against Aristotle's logic, but you cannot deny reality. Reality is reality! You can change the logic – which is man-made – but you cannot change the behavior of electrons. It is not in your power, it is existential. So a non-Aristotelian logic has grown up.

The second case was geometry. Euclid reigned for hundreds of years as a perfect master as far as geometry is concerned, but in the last century that too has got into trouble. Non-Euclidian geometries have evolved. They had to be evolved because of the new discoveries of physics. For example, you have heard that the closest distance between two points makes a straight line, but the discovery of the physicists is that there is no straight line at all. A straight line is impossible, for the simple reason that you are sitting on a global earth. You can draw a straight line here on the floor, but it is not a straight line because it is part of a circle. If you go on drawing it from both ends, one day they will meet somewhere and you will see that it has become a circle. So the small piece that you were thinking was a straight line was not a straight line; it is just that it was such a small part of a circle that you could not see the curve. The curve was so small that it was all but invisible – but it was there. In the same way, everything from Euclid has been cancelled.

Patanjali remains the only person yet, and perhaps may remain the only person, who has created a whole science alone, and has remained for five thousand years without any challenge from any corner. He calls it the *turiya*, the fourth. He is so scientific a man that one simply feels amazed.

Five thousand years ago, he had the courage, the insight, the awareness, to say that God is only a hypothesis. It can help you to become awakened but it is not a reality, it is only a device. There is no God to be achieved; it is only a hypothesis.

A few people can be helped by hypotheses – they can use the hypothesis of God – but remember, it is not a reality. And once you have become awakened it disappears, the same way as when you wake up your dreams disappear. They were so real that sometimes it happens that even after you have awakened there are some effects remaining of the reality of the dream: your heart is beating faster, you are perspiring, trembling, still afraid. Now you know perfectly it was a dream, but you are still crying, your tears are there. The dream was non-existential, but it has affected you because for that period you had taken it to be real.

So it is possible. You can see the devotees crying before their god, emotionally very much affected, dancing, singing, worshipping, and feeling the truth of it, but it is just a hypothesis. There is nothing, no God, but these people are taking the hypothesis as a reality. One day when they are awake they will laugh at themselves, seeing that it was only a hypothesis.

But there are other masters who have given different names according to their own philosophical background. A few have called it enlightenment, becoming full of light – all darkness disappears, all unconsciousness disappears – becoming fully conscious.

There are others who have called it liberation, freedom – freedom from yourself, remember. All other freedoms are political, social. They are freedom from somebody, from some government, from some country, from some political party; but it is always freedom *from* . . . Religious freedom is freedom not from somebody else, but from yourself.

You are no more.

Because you are no more, a few masters in the East have called it *anatta* – no-selfness. Buddha called it *nirvana* – which is very close to *anatta*, no-selfness, or selflessness – just a zero, a profound nothingness surrounding you. But it is not emptiness, it is fullness: fullness of being, of ultimate joy, fullness of being blessed, fullness of gracefulness. All that you have known before is no longer there; hence it is empty of all that. But something new, absolutely new you had not even dreamt about, is discovered.

Some have called it universal existence. But what name you give does not matter. I think "the fourth" remains the best, because it does not lead you into mind trips; otherwise you are going to think about it, "What is emptiness? What is nothingness?" And nothingness can create a fear, emptiness can create a fear, *anatta*, no-selfness, can create a fear. "The fourth" is absolutely right.

Three stages you know; the fourth is just a little deeper. It is not far away. The idea of being so far away, so many lives away from it, is a dream. In reality it is just by the side . . . wake up and you are it.

I just want to be ordinary and happy. I want a woman to love, and to love me; friends to spend time with and enjoy. I don't want enlightenment. Have I come to the wrong place?

Centuries of wrong upbringing have completely confused your mind about enlightenment. The very word seems to be unearthly, otherworldly; the very word seems to be something which is after death, or for those who are already dead. This is absolutely wrong.

If you want to be happy there is no other way than enlightenment. If you want to be ordinary, nobody has ever been ordinary without enlightenment. If you want to love and be loved it is impossible without enlightenment. So you will have to understand my concept of enlightenment. It is just to be ordinary, healthy, aware, whole, total.

Every mind is seeking some extraordinariness. That is what the ego is: always trying to be somebody in particular, always afraid of being nobody, always afraid of emptiness, always trying to fill the inner void with anything and everything.

Every human being is seeking extraordinariness – and that creates misery. It is not possible. Nobodiness is your very nature, non-being is the very stuff you are made of. However you try you will never succeed; even Alexanders fail. You cannot be somebody because that is not possible in the nature of things. You can only be nobody. But there is nothing wrong in being nobody; in fact, the moment you accept your nobodiness, immediately bliss starts flowing from you in all directions – because misery disappears.

Misery is the shadow of the ego, the shadow of the ambitious mind. Misery means you are doing something impossible and because you are failing in it you are miserable. You are doing something unnatural, trying to do it and failing, so you feel frustrated, miserable.

Hell is nothing but the end result of an impossible, unnatural effort. Heaven is nothing but to be natural.

You are nobody. You are born as a nobodiness with no name, no form. You will die as a nobody. Name and form are just on the surface; deep down you are just a vast space. And it is beautiful, because if you are somebody you will be limited. It is good that existence doesn't allow anybody to be "somebody". If you are somebody you will be finite, limited, you will be an imprisoned being. No, existence doesn't allow that. It gives you the freedom of nobodiness, infinite, non-ending. But you are not ready.

To me, enlightenment is all about this phenomenon: to recognize, to realize, to accept the fact that one is a nobody. Suddenly you stop trying the impossible. Suddenly you stop pulling yourself up by your shoelaces. You understand the absurdity of it – and you stop. And laughter spreads over your being. Suddenly you are calm and collected. The very effort of wanting to be somebody is creating trouble.

And when you try to be somebody, you cannot love. An ambitious mind cannot love. It is impossible, because you first have to fulfil your ambition. An ambitious mind has to sacrifice everything for the ambition; you will go on sacrificing your love. Look at ambitious people – if they are after money they always postpone love. Tomorrow, when they have accumulated a lot of money, then they will be in love; right now it is impossible, it is not in any way practical; right now they cannot afford it. Love is a relaxation and they are running after something to achieve, a goal. Maybe it is money, maybe it is power, prestige, politics. How can they love now? They cannot be here and now – and love is a phenomenon of here and now. Love exists only in the present, ambition exists in the future. Love and ambition never meet.

You cannot love – and if you cannot love, how can you be loved by anybody else? Love is a deep communion of two beings who are ready to be together – this moment, not tomorrow; who are ready to be total in this moment and forget all past and future. Love is a forgetfulness of the past and the future and a remembrance of this moment, this throbbing moment, this alive moment. Love is the truth of the moment.

The ambitious mind is never here, he is always on the go. How can you love a running man? He is always in a race, in a competition; he has no time. Or he thinks that somewhere in the future, when the goal is achieved, when he has attained the power he seeks, the riches he desires, then he will relax and love. This is not going to happen, because the goal will never be achieved.

Ambition will never be fulfilled. It is not the nature of it to be fulfilled. You can fulfil one ambition; immediately a thousand other ambitions arise out of it. Ambition never stops.

If you follow it, if you understand, it can stop right now. But if you give energy to it, how can you love? That's why people are so miserable trying to be somebody – miserable because they are not getting love, miserable because they cannot love.

Love is an ecstasy: ecstasy of a no-mind, ecstasy of the present, ecstasy of a non-ambitious state, ecstasy of emptiness. Wherever lovers are, there is nobody: only love exists. When two lovers meet, they are not two. They may appear two to you, from the outside. But the inside story is totally different: they are not two. The moment they meet the two-ness disappears, only love exists and flows. How is it possible unless you are an emptiness within, a nothingness, so that there is no barrier, nothing between you and your lover? If you are somebody, and your lover or beloved is also somebody, then two persons are not meeting but four: two real nobodies, who are standing in the background, and two somebodies – false egos shaking hands, caressing, making gestures of love. It is a drama to look at, ridiculous!

Whenever lovers meet, there is nobody, and two nobodies cannot be two. How can two nothingnesses be two? Nothingnesses have no demarcation line – a nothingness is a vastness. Two nothingnesses become one. Two somebodies remain two.

That's why love becomes such an ugly affair – the love that is called love by you, not by me. Your love is an ugly affair, it has to be so. It could have been the most beautiful phenomenon in the world but it has become the ugliest, with lovers constantly fighting, quarrelling, creating misery for each other. Sartre says, "The other is hell." He is saying something about your love. Whenever you are alone you feel relaxed, whenever you are with the lover a tension arises. You cannot live alone, because the deepest nobodiness hankers to be filled; it has a thirst, a deep hunger. So you cannot remain alone. You have to move – you seek togetherness, but the moment you are together it is a misery.

All relationships create misery and nothing else. Unless you are enlightened, love becomes just a conflict, a quarrel. One, by and by, gets adjusted to it. That means one, by and by, gets dull, insensitive. That's why the whole world looks so dead, so stale. It stinks. All relationships have gone stale, they have become ugly.

So if you want really to love and be loved, it is not possible right now as you are. You have to disappear. You have to leave, so that a clean nothingness is left, a fresh nothingness is left behind. Only then can the flower of love bloom. The seeds are there but the ego is like a rock, and the seeds cannot sprout on it.

You say you want to be ordinary, and you want to love, and you want friends, you want to enjoy? This is exactly what enlightenment is all about! But if you go to the priests and to the preachers and to the organized religions and the churches, their enlightenment is different. They are against love; they are against ordinariness. They are against friendship, they are against enjoyment; they are against everything that your nature naturally seeks. They are the great poisoners.

But if you have come to me you have come to the right person – the right person in the sense that my enlightenment is of this world.

I'm not saying that there is no other world. I am not saying that the earthly existence is the only existence – no. Don't misunderstand me. But the other depends on this, the other world depends on this world, and the sky depends on this earth. If you want to move higher you have to be rooted deeper here in this earth. You need roots in this life, then flowers will come in the other life. The other life is not against this life; in fact, the other life is just the flowering of this life. The divine is not against the world, godliness is not outside it; it is hidden within this world. You need not go against the world to seek fulfilment – if you go you will never find it. It is hidden here and now. You have to seek, you have to go deep into this existence – and that is the only way to find it. This whole life, this whole existence is nothing but a temple, and the divine is hiding inside it. Don't escape from it.

I am not against this life; in fact I am not against anything. I am for everything, because if it exists there must be a purpose to it. God cannot create things without any purpose – he is not mad. Existence is very purposeful, meaningful; if this life exists it means the other life cannot exist without it. It is the base.

But you carry your notions when you come to me. When you come to me and I talk about enlightenment, you understand me in terms of what you have been taught about enlightenment. When you come to me and I talk about renunciation, *sannyas*, you understand something else, not what I am saying. I have to use your language, and the words are all contaminated. They have been used millions of times by millions of people with different connotations, different meanings, and I am giving them different dimensions of meaning.

Enlightenment is one who is fully aware of his inner emptiness and is not fighting it; rather, he enjoys it, it is blissful. Through the enjoyment of his own emptiness he becomes available to others. Others can enjoy, others can come and participate in his mystery. His doors are open, he invites friends and lovers, and he is ready to share, he is ready to give. When you give out of your emptiness you are never afraid of giving because you cannot exhaust the emptiness.

You go on giving, you go on giving, you go on giving – it is always there, you cannot exhaust it.

Only finite things can be exhausted, that's why they create miserliness – you are afraid to give. But a man who knows he is empty, why should he be afraid to give? He can give himself totally – and unless that is possible, love is not possible. Love is a holy phenomenon, love is not profane. Every love worth the name is sacred. And when you enter into love you enter into the world of purity, innocence. When you love you enter the temple of the divine.

Enjoy! I am not for sadness and long faces. I am not here to make you more miserable – you are already too miserable. I am not here to give you more sadness. I am here to awaken you to the bliss that is your birthright, that is naturally available to you. But you have forgotten how to approach it, and you are going in wrong directions. You seek it somewhere where it is not; you seek it outside and it is inside. You seek it far away and it is near; you seek it in the distant stars and it is just in front of you.

In English there are two words that are beautiful. One is "obvious" – obvious means just in front of you. It comes from a Latin root meaning just in front of you. And then there is another word, "problem". It comes from a Greek root which also means just in front of you. The root meaning of "obvious" and "problem" is the same. The obvious is the problem, that which is just in front of you is the problem – you cannot see it, because your eyes are wandering into distant lands. The obvious has become the problem.

Enlightenment is to become aware of the obvious, and when you become aware of the obvious the problem disappears.

To live a life of no problems is to live an enlightened life. It is a totally different way of being. It has nothing to do with achievement, it has nothing to do with learning, it has nothing to do with effort, practice. The only thing that is needed is to be a little more alert so that you can look at, see, watch that which is in front of you. The solution is closer, very much closer to you than you can imagine. Don't seek it far away; it exists within you. Once you are settled inside, centred, rooted, then you have all freedom – go, and love. Go and be in the world; now you will be able to enjoy it, you will be able to taste it, you will be able to penetrate into its deepest possibilities. And whenever you enter into the realms of depth, always you will find the divine there. In love, go deep and you will find godliness; in food, eat well, with alertness, awareness, and you will find the divine.

The Upanishads say *Annam Brahm* – food is God. And the Upanishads say that sex is just a brother, a twin brother of the final, ultimate bliss. A twin brother of the ultimate final bliss is sex! You have condemned it so much. It may be the lowest rung of the ladder, but it belongs to the ladder. The highest rung belongs as much as the lowest; in fact, everything belongs to God and is divine.

This is enlightenment: to be able to see the sacred throbbing within. Real religion is not against anything, real religion is the search to find the holy everywhere. And it is there, waiting for you.

You have come to the right place. Your mind may like to escape from here, because this is going to be a death to your mind. It is the right place for you, but the wrong place for the mind. It is the absolutely right place for your being – but for your ambitions, your ego, your pride, your stupidities, it is the most wrong place you can find anywhere on the earth at this moment.

So you decide. If you want to be stupid, escape. Then the mind will go on befooling you that you are in love and enjoying – and you know you are not enjoying, and you know that you are not in love. Then the mind may go on befooling you that you are indulging – you cannot indulge. You are not even there to indulge. You don't exist, you don't have an integrated being in any way. You may wander around and deceive yourself but if you really want to be loved by a woman and you want a woman to love, and you want friends, and you want to enjoy life – I am giving you the keys to it.

Now or Never

What is this enlightenment all about? What do you understand by enlightenment?

The first thing is that it can never be in the future. You cannot make a goal of it; it can never be tomorrow. Either it is here and now, or never. Remember those words, now or never!

Many people have misunderstood the idea of enlightenment. The idea of enlightenment is to remain in the present moment. I call it meditation. Not to go into the past, which is no more, and not to go into the future, which is not yet – because if you go into past and future, you are going to miss the present moment, which is the only reality.

Just be here, now. And if you are here and now, enlightenment comes of its own accord. It is not a goal that you have to reach. It is not somewhere far away, so that you have to travel a path to it. It comes to you, you never go to it. It is not your doing, it is a happening.

All that you have to understand is to be authentically in the present, because there is no other reality anywhere. This small moment, this silence – and suddenly you will feel something arising from the very depths of your being. It has always been there; you never gave it a chance. You have been wandering everywhere, but you have not allowed your innermost core just a little space, a little time.

All the religions teach you that God is *there* – far away. You need a saviour, a messiah, a prophet, a holy book, a religion, to help you to reach *there*. They teach you that heaven is far away, and you have to accumulate virtue to deserve it. They keep your eyes focused on a faraway future. And in this way, life goes on slipping out of your hands. From the cradle to the grave you are just hoping and hoping and hoping . . . and what comes is neither God nor heaven, but death! Meanwhile you missed the tremendous opportunity of being alive. You simply vegetated, because you were not interested in life itself.

One Christian theologian, a great intellectual, respected all over the world, was Stanley Jones. He was travelling all around the world, preaching the gospel of Christ.

I met him in one of his discourses, and afterwards I spoke to him. I said, "Your discourse was beautiful, but do you understand what you are doing? You are harming all these simple people. You are proving exactly what Karl Marx used to say, that religions are nothing but opium to the people. I don't agree with Karl Marx on anything else, but on this statement I cannot disagree. You are giving them dreams of the future, of an eternal life beyond death. Have you been beyond death?

"Being a Christian, certainly you cannot say that you have been beyond death. A Hindu may be able to say yes, because he believes in many lives. He can say that he has been through the process of death many times, but you cannot say that. Christians, Jews, Mohammedans believe only in one life, so there is going to be only one death. Have you been beyond death? Have you come to speak to these people having experienced what you are saying?"

I asked him, "Be sincere. I hope that you will be honest. And if you don't know what is beyond death, then why destroy these people's lives? Focusing their mind on the future, which is unknown, is really murderous. In my eyes, you are not a theologian but a murderer! The law may not charge you as a murderer but you cannot deny that you have murdered many people; you have taken them away from the present – and that is the only life there is."

Live this moment in its totality. All your organized religions have goals. But this is not a religion, this is a mystery school. This is a *religio*, the root from where the word "religion" has come. *Religio* means putting you together. Nothing else – no God, no heaven, no hell, just putting you together, a crystallization. And that can happen only in the present.

I don't sell opium, I am not a dope dealer. For that you will have to go to Christian bishops and cardinals and the Pope – they are dope dealers. The dope is so subtle that the law cannot catch them; it is invisible. But it is far more dangerous than the ordinary dope. Once you get accustomed to focusing your life, your longing, your hope, in the future, you are finished. You have committed suicide, you will not be able to live.

I teach you life. I teach you love. I teach you meditation. They all mean the same thing: to be in the present. And see the beauty of being in the present – the silence that descends, the serenity that surrounds you, a tremendous contentment that arises for no reason at all.

And as you become more and more attuned to the present, as your depth within yourself grows, suddenly one fine morning you really wake up! Not the everyday waking – you *really* wake up, because you are at your very centre, and you see the whole of life in a new light. The whole existence becomes luminous. Everything becomes a glory unto itself. Small things start having tremendous meaning. You have done what God had forbidden in the Bible; you have eaten the fruit of wisdom and the fruit of eternal life. Now you know those trees are not outside you, they are your very being.

The Garden of Eden is not somewhere outside, it is within you. And once it is felt, what a relief, what a blessing!

This I call enlightenment.

Then, moment to moment, you go on growing more and more into light, into life, into love. There is no end to it. Even the sky is not the end. You are far bigger than the whole universe. You are carrying within yourself all the millions of stars, all the flowers, all the music of the world. There is nothing that you are missing.

This experience I call enlightenment.

But please, don't make it a goal; otherwise you will miss it. Make it a goal and you have missed it. You simply learn how to be in the present, and enlightenment comes to you. You don't have to go anywhere.

Part II

DIALOGUES AND DEFINITIONS

In Search of a Science of the Soul

When I talk about the psychology of the buddhas, one thing
to be remembered is that it is not really a psychology. I have
to use words. No word is adequate for it but I have to use
some words – but always take them with a pinch of salt. It
cannot really be called a psychology. Psychology presupposes
a mind and Buddha is a no-mind. Psychology presupposes
that the mind is functioning, thinking, planning, worrying,
imagining, dreaming – and a buddha has no dreaming, no
planning, no worrying, no thinking. He simply exists. He
exists like a rock, like a tree, like a river – with just one
difference, a tremendous difference. The difference is that
he exists without mind but full of awareness.

This awareness cannot be understood from the outside.
If you try to understand it you will only misunderstand it.
There is no way to check it with instruments, there is no
way. It will not appear on any graph. All that can appear on
a graph remains of the mind, it is not of the beyond. The
beyond is beyond grasp. One has to become a buddha, one
has to become the awakened soul, one has to come to this
awareness oneself.

Your Mind Is Not Yours

The mind is within you, but it is really a projection of the society inside you. It is not yours.

No child is born with a mind. He is born with a brain. The brain is the mechanism; the mind is the ideology. The brain is fed by the society, and every society creates a mind according to its own conditionings. That's why there are so many minds in the world. The Hindu mind is certainly separate from the Christian mind, and the communist mind is certainly separate from the Buddhist mind.

But a fallacy is created in the individual that the mind is yours, so the individual starts acting according to the society, following the society, but feeling as if he is functioning on his own.

Your mind is not your mind – this is something basic to be remembered. Your mind is an implantation of the society in which you have accidentally been born. If you had been born in a Christian home but had been immediately transferred to a Mohammedan family and brought up by the Mohammedans, you would not have the same mind as you do now. You would have a totally different mind, so different that you cannot conceive of it.

Bertrand Russell, one of the geniuses of our times, tried hard to get rid of the Christian mind – not because it was Christian, but simply because it was given to him by others. He wanted his own fresh outlook about things. He did not want to see things through somebody else's glasses; he wanted to come in contact with reality immediately and directly. He wanted his own mind. So it was not a question of his being against the Christian mind; if he had been a Hindu he would have done the same, if he had been a Mohammedan he would have done the same, if he had been a communist he would have done the same.

The question is whether the mind is your own or implanted by others – because others implant a mind in you that does not serve you, but serves their own purposes.

For years in the Soviet Union, each child was brought up with a communist mind. One of my friends, Rahul Sankritayana, was visiting the Soviet Union and went to visit a school. He asked a small boy there, "Do you believe in God?" The boy looked at him in shock and he said, "At your age, in this century, you ask such a question! In the past when people were ignorant they used to believe in God. There is no God." Now this child will believe for his whole life that this is his voice speaking. It is not so. It is the voice of the society, and it serves the purposes of the vested interests of that society.

You are prepared by the parents, by the teachers, by the priests, by your educational system to have a certain kind of mind, and your whole life you go on living through that certain kind of mind. That is a borrowed life. And that is why there is so much misery in the world: because nobody is living authentically, nobody is living his own self; he is simply following orders implanted in him.

Bertrand Russell tried hard to get rid of this implanted mind, and wrote a book, *Why I Am Not a Christian*. But in a letter to a friend he wrote, "Although I have written the book, and although I do not believe that I am a Christian, that I have dropped that mind, still, deep down it persists. One day I asked myself, 'Who is the greatest man in history?' Rationally I know it is Gautam Buddha, but I could not put Gautam Buddha above Jesus Christ.

"That day I felt that all my efforts have been futile. I am still a Christian. I know rationally that Jesus Christ stands no comparison with Gautam Buddha – but it is only rational. Emotionally, sentimentally I cannot put Gautam Buddha above Jesus Christ. Jesus Christ remains in my unconscious, still affecting my attitudes, my approaches, my behavior. The world thinks I am no longer a Christian, but I know . . . It seems difficult to get rid of this mind! They have cultivated it with such acumen, with such craftsmanship."

And it is a long process. You never think about it. A man lives 75 years, and for 20 years he has to be in schools, colleges, the university; one third of his life is devoted to cultivating a certain mind.

Bertrand Russell failed because he had no knowledge of how to get rid of it. He was fighting, but he was groping in the dark. There are absolutely certain methods of meditation that can take you away from the mind, and then it is very easy if you want to drop it. But without first becoming separate from the mind it is impossible to drop it – who is going to drop whom? Bertrand Russell is fighting with one half of his mind against the other half, and both are Christian – it is impossible!

And now it has been proved scientifically. One of the most important scientific contributions is from Delgado. He found seven hundred centres in the brain. Each centre is capable of containing an immense quantity of knowledge; it is just like a recording. And his experiments are shocking: he touches a certain centre in the brain with an electrode, and the person starts speaking. He takes away the electrode and the person stops. He puts the electrode back on the same centre, and the person starts speaking again – from the very beginning.

Delgado himself was not able to figure out how the tape gets rewound – because the person would always start from the beginning. Wherever you left off makes no difference; it was not that the person would resume speaking from the point where you left him. Whatever automatic process exists in the mind that causes the person to start again from the beginning has yet be discovered.

But it was discovered that an electrode can be implanted in the brain, and it can be triggered by remote control. Delgado exhibited it in Spain, in a bullfight. He planted an electrode in the brain of the toughest bull, and then stood in the field waving a red flag. The bull rushed toward him ferociously, and the people almost stopped breathing: "The bull is going to kill one of our best geniuses!" But they did not know that he had a remote control switch in his pocket – just a small box with a switch.

When the bull was about to attack, from just a few inches away, Delgado pushed the button and the bull stopped, frozen. And he did it many times – again and again the bull would come with the same ferocity, and again and again he would stop whenever Delgado pushed the button.

Delgado says, "Sooner or later, this discovery can either become a blessing to humanity, or it can become a curse."

Every child's mind could be easily implanted with an electrode. Then you would have very obedient people; you would not have any rebels, you would not have any revolutionaries – but the whole charm of life will be gone! People will be simply vegetables, enslaved scientifically. And they will not know, because the remote control unit might be in the capital, in the hands of the government.

This kind of technology can be useful – criminals can be prevented, murderers can be prevented, thieves can be changed, rapists can be transformed – but it is dangerous also. Anybody who is in power can make the whole country just a crowd of slaves. And you cannot do anything, because you don't know. Remember that inside the skull, where the brain is, you don't have any sensitivity. Even if a stone is put inside your skull, you will never know; you just don't have sensitive nerves there which can inform you.

Delgado's mechanism is scientific, but society has been doing the same by planting ideas . . . It is an old bullock-cart method. It takes so long, 25 years, and it is not foolproof, because a few revolutionaries escape, a few rebels are still born. And it is good that there are people who escape from the enslaving structure of the society, because these are the people who have advanced knowledge, who have given us all the scientific progress, who have challenged all the old superstitions.

But the society wants you simply to be a carbon copy, never an original.

The method used to create a certain type of mind in you is to go on repeating certain things continuously. And if a lie is repeated continuously it starts becoming a truth; you forget that it was a lie in the beginning.

Adolf Hitler started lying to the German people that all the misery of their country was because of the Jews. Now this is such an absurd thing – like somebody saying that all the misery of the country is because of bicycles, so if we destroy all the bicycles all the misery will disappear. In fact the Jews were the very backbone of Germany, they had created all the country's wealth. And the Jews had no nation of their own, so any nation, wherever they were, was their nation. They had no other alternative in their minds; they could not betray, and they were doing all the things that any German was doing for the welfare of the country.

But Adolf Hitler in his autobiography writes, "It doesn't matter what you say, because there is no such thing as truth. Truth is a lie that has been repeated so often that you have forgotten that it is a lie." So the only difference, according to him, between truth and a lie is that the lie is fresh and truth is old; otherwise there is no difference. And his statement seems to carry some insight.

For example, Christianity, Hinduism, Mohammedanism – these three religions repeat to their children that there is a God. Jainism, Buddhism, Taoism, three other religions, all say there is no God. The first group of three religions have a certain mind, and their lives are filled with the idea of God, hell, heaven, prayer. The second group of three religions has no prayer because there is nobody to pray to, there is no God. The very question does not arise.

In communist countries they don't believe even in the soul of man, and every child is continually told that man is matter, that when a man dies he simply dies, nothing remains; that there is no soul and consciousness is a by-product. Now every communist repeats it as the truth.

Adolf Hitler cannot be accused of being absolutely absurd. It seems to be the case that if you repeat anything to people, they will slowly, slowly start believing it. And if it has been repeated for centuries, it has become a heritage.

Your mind is not yours. And your mind is not young; it is centuries old – three thousand years old, five thousand years old.

I want you to understand that it is not your mind, and your search should be to find your own mind. To be under somebody else's influence is to remain psychologically a slave. And life is not for slavery. It is to taste freedom.

There is something like truth, but with the mind you have you can never know it – because this mind is full of lies, repeated century after century. You can find the truth when you put this mind completely aside and look at existence with fresh eyes, like a newborn child; then, whatever you experience is truth. And if you remain constantly alert not to allow others to interfere with your inner growth, there comes a moment when you become so attuned with existence, so one with existence . . .

Only this experience is religious experience. It is not Jewish, it is not Christian, it is not Hindu. How can any experience be Jewish, Hindu or Mohammedan? You never see the ridiculousness of the very idea. You eat something and you say it is delicious, but is it Christian, or Hindu, or Buddhist? You taste something and you say it is sweet, but is it communist? – is it materialist or spiritual? These questions are nonsense. It is simply sweet, it is simply delicious.

When you feel existence immediately, without any mediator, with no mind given by anybody else to you, you taste something which transforms you, which makes you enlightened, awakened, which brings you to the highest peak of consciousness.

A greater fulfilment there is not. A higher contentment there is not. A deeper relaxation there is not.

You have come home.

Life becomes a joy, a song, a dance, a celebration. I call this life religious.

I want everybody to be religious, but I don't want anybody to be Christian, Hindu, Mohammedan – because those are the barriers which will never allow you to become religious. And you can see it clearly: Gautam Buddha is not a Buddhist, he never heard the word Buddhist; Jesus Christ is not a Christian, he never heard the word Christian and certainly he is not a Jew; otherwise Jews would not have crucified him. If Jews decided to crucify Jesus, that simply means he had dropped the mind that they had given him to carry for his whole life, that he was saying things that were not part of their given mind.

And Jesus continuously reminds them of it. He says, "It has been said by the old prophets" – and who were those old prophets? They were all Jews – "it has been said, 'An eye for an eye is the law.' But I say unto you that if somebody slaps you on one cheek, give him the other cheek, too." This was not part of the Jewish mind. The Jewish God declares, "I am not a nice person! I am a very angry God, I am very jealous. Remember that I am not your uncle." These are actually the words: "I am not your uncle, I am not nice, I am jealous, I am angry." And Jesus says, "God is love."

I am trying to show you that Jesus had dropped the Jewish mind, and the reward he got was crucifixion. The crucifixion was the reward for dropping the Jewish mind. He was dangerous in the sense that he would create doubt in other people's minds: "Our God says he is angry, jealous – he will destroy those who are against him, and Jesus is saying that God is love. He is going against our vested interest."

He was killed – he was not a Jew. He was not Christian because the word "Christian" does not exist in the Hebrew language; the word "Christ" does not exist in the Hebrew language. He was called the messiah – that is equivalent to "Christ". "Christ" is a Greek word. It was three hundred years later that Jesus' sayings were translated into Greek; then messiah became Christ, and the followers became Christians.

Gautam Buddha was not a Hindu. He was born in a Hindu family, but he renounced it; he renounced it the very day he started his search for truth. See the simple point: the Hindu need not search for the truth; the Hindu has already got it ready-made. It has been given to him by the tradition, by the religion, by the scriptures; he need not go in search. The day Gautam Buddha went in search for truth, he dropped the Hindu mind. And of course he was not a Buddhist; that was a name his followers were given later on by Hindus, to make the distinction. But Buddha had his own mind.

To have one's own mind in the world is the richest thing possible. But no society allows it; every society keeps you poor. On your account every society, particularly those who are in power – through money or through politics, through religion or through knowledge, for any reason – those who are in power don't want people to have their own minds. It is dangerous to their interests. They want not human beings but sheep, not individuals but crowds, who are always in need of being led, who are always in need of being told what to do, what not to do; who don't have their own minds, their own insights, their own consciousness. They are always dependent.

The fear of anybody being different, being a stranger, being an outsider, is always the same for a simple reason. No society will have the courage to accept you if that society has not created your mind, because that society cannot trust that you will always be obedient, that you will never object or create doubt about anything, or be sceptical about anything.

No society wants strangers, outsiders. Why is the whole world afraid of me? I am not a terrorist; I am not making bombs and killing people. I am a non-violent person. But they can accept terrorists.

In Germany it actually happened . . . The government prevented me from entering Germany, passed a resolution saying that I am a dangerous man and I should not be allowed entry into Germany, and at the same time they allowed all the terrorist groups of Europe to have a world conference there. I was simply amazed! All the terrorist groups that have been murdering people, that have hijacked airplanes, that have bombed embassies, that have kidnapped people – their international conference was allowed, but I could not be allowed four weeks as a tourist in the country.

But those terrorists are not of a different mind from the mind of the German society.

It is a strange phenomenon. Three people were being crucified the same day as Jesus, and it was the convention that one could be forgiven – and it was the people's decision. Pontius Pilate was absolutely certain that they would ask to release Jesus. Jesus was innocent; he had done no harm to anybody. But the whole crowd shouted, "We want Barabbas" – and Barabbas was a confirmed criminal. He had committed murders, rapes . . . any kind of crime you could name he had done it.

But you should not be surprised, because Barabbas belonged to the Jews. He may have been a murderer, but his mind was still that of a Jew. This Jesus might be innocent, but his mind is no longer that of the Jews; he is an outsider, he is dangerous. Barabbas is not dangerous. What can he do? A few more murders at the most. But this Jesus can destroy the whole structure of the society, because it is standing only on superstitions.

Even Barabbas could not believe it. He thought something must have gone wrong: "There is not another criminal in the whole country who can compete with me, and this poor Jesus, who has never done anything except talk to few people here and there . . . And nobody is asking for him to be released." Not a single voice shouted for Jesus to be released, and thousands of people shouted, "Barabbas! We want Barabbas!"

If you go into the psychology of it, it is very simple. All those terrorists having a conference in Germany are acceptable: they have the same mind, the same politics. They belong to the same rotten society. But I cannot be allowed; they have the idea that I will corrupt people. The same was the condemnation of Socrates, that he corrupts people – and all that Socrates was doing was teaching people to have their own mind.

All the great masters in the world have been saying only one thing down the centuries, "Have your own mind and have your own individuality. Don't be a part of the crowd; don't be a wheel in the whole mechanism of a vast society. Be individual, on your own. Live life with your own eyes; listen to music with your own ears."

But we are not doing anything with our own ears, with our own eyes, with our own minds; everything is being taught, and we are following it.

Deviation is dangerous to the rotten societies. And particularly in the West – where no idea of enlightenment has ever existed – it is more so, because enlightenment simply means going beyond the mind. And going beyond the mind you will be yourself.

The West has never nourished the idea of enlightenment. It is against the society, against the religion; they have never bothered about it.

Think about truth – that is allowed. That's why in the West philosophy has grown to great heights and depths. But it is always *thinking* about truth. It is like madmen thinking about sanity, blind men thinking about light. However the blind man tries to think about light – he may create a big system of thought about what light is – it is not going to be anything like light. For light, you need eyes.

You cannot think about truth, because thinking will be done by your mind – which is full of lies, nothing but lies. How are you going to think about truth? Truth can be found only when you have put the mind aside.

In the East we say truth is the experience that happens in the state of no-mind, or in the state of beyond mind. But in the West the very idea has not existed. And that will make one thing clear to you: philosophy is a Western thing. In the East there is nothing like philosophy.

It is very strange: the Eastern civilization is far older, at least ten thousand years old, but there is nothing like philosophy in the East. What is called Eastern philosophy is a wrong name. In the East it is called *darshan – darshan* means "to see". It has nothing to do with thinking; the very word *darshan* means "to see".

I call it *philosia*, as against philosophy, because philosophy means "to think", and *philosia* means "the love of seeing". Philosophy means "the love of thinking" – but what can you think? Just to avoid the danger of people going beyond mind, and becoming dangerous to the society, a substitute, a toy has been created. That is philosophy.

No philosopher comes to experience anything. No philosopher becomes enlightened or awakened; he remains on the same ground as you are, as unconscious as you are.

Darshan, philosia, is a totally different approach. Its approach is through witnessing your mind – not by thinking but just becoming a watcher of your mind and creating a distance between you and your thoughts. Just seeing them, as if you are on a hill and the whole mind and its traffic is going on down in the valley, a moment comes when thoughts start disappearing, because their life is in your identification with them. Their life is the life of a parasite; they suck your blood. If you are far away and you are not giving any juice to your thoughts, they start shrinking and dying. And when there are no thoughts around you but immense silence, tremendous nothingness, just a watcher and nothing to watch . . . this is the moment you are freed from the fetters of the mind. And this is the moment of the beginning of a new life.

But you may look mad to people, because from this moment your behavior will be different. From this moment you will have an originality; you cannot be part of the crowd. People will think you have gone wrong somewhere. It is strange – because it is these people who are wrong! But in a way it is not so strange. If you have eyes and you go into a society of blind people, nobody is going to believe that you have eyes. You must be suffering from some mad illusion, because eyes don't exist. Nobody has eyes; how can you have?

The enlightened person in the West will be condemned as mad.

The people who are mad in the West are mad because you have created so much tension and anxiety and anguish, and you have given them such a rotten mind that it cannot manage. A point comes when it breaks down. When the mind breaks down, the person falls below the mind; hence psychoanalysis is a Western phenomenon. In the East there is nothing parallel to psychoanalysis.

In the East we have worked for a break*through*, not for a breakdown. The breakthrough takes you above the mind, and the breakdown simply pulls you to a subhuman level. But for that, too, society is responsible. It gives you too much ambition, which it cannot fulfil. It gives you too much desire – for money, for power – which it cannot fulfil. It only teaches you how to go on climbing the ladder of success, higher and higher, and tells you to be quick because you have only a small life, and so much has to be done! There is no time for living, no time for loving, no time for rejoicing.

People go on postponing everything that is meaningful. Tomorrow they will laugh; today, money has to be gathered . . . more money, more power, more things, more gadgets. Tomorrow they will love; today there is no time. But tomorrow never comes, and one day they find themselves burdened with all kinds of gadgets, burdened with money, they have come to the top of the ladder – and there is nowhere to go except to jump in a lake. But they cannot even say to other people, "Don't bother to come here – there is nothing", because that will make them look stupid. You have become the president of the country and you are saying, "Here is nothing, so don't bother. This is simply a ladder that leads nowhere"? You will feel stupid.

So people go on pretending that they have achieved, that they have found, and deep down they are feeling empty, meaningless, and as if they have wasted their whole life. If they break down under such pressure, the society is responsible. The society is driving people mad.

In the East you will not find so many mad people, so many people committing suicide – and the East is poor, so poor that people can't manage to have one meal a day. Logically there should be more people committing suicide, more people going mad. But no, they are not going mad, they are not committing suicide. They seem to live in a certain contentment, because ambition is not part of the mind given by the society. Their society also gives them ambition, but for the other world, not for this world. This world is condemned.

Try to understand it . . . The Eastern society also gives people ambition – ambition to reach paradise, to realize God – but that ambition is against the ambitions of this world. It says, "Renounce this world! Here there is nothing but shadows; it is illusory." For thousands of years people have thought this world is illusory, it is worthless to bother about it – why not look for the real thing? So they don't go mad. Even in utter poverty, in sickness, in death you will not find them tense or anxious, and they don't need any psychotherapy.

Psychotherapy is absolutely Western; it is the need of the Western mind. First the Western mind creates all kinds of desires and ambitions, which are going to create a breakdown sooner or later, and then psychotherapy comes in. It is now the most highly paid profession – but the strangest thing is that psychotherapists commit suicide more than people from any other profession, twice as much, and psychotherapists go mad twice as often as people in any other profession. And these are the people who are helping others to be sane? It is really a mess.

It can be cleaned up. It is simply a question of understanding that the mind that we have is not capable of encountering reality, because reality is contemporary and the mind is two thousand years old. The gap is big, and the mind fails to encounter reality. The mind has to go with reality, step by step; it has not to lag behind. And that is possible only if each individual has his own mind, his own individuality.

I am basically an individualist, because only the individual has a soul. No group can claim a soul; they are all dead arrangements. Only the individual is a living phenomenon. We have to help the living phenomenon to be contemporary

– and to remain contemporary, because what is contemporary today will not be contemporary tomorrow. So you have to learn the methods of flowing like a river with existence, each moment. Die each moment to the past, and be born each moment to the new.

Unless that becomes your religion, you are going to be in trouble, and your society is going to be in trouble.

Why can modern psychologists not think or write about or even conceive of enlightenment? Is enlightenment a new phenomenon beyond their conception? Will they ever understand a phenomenon beyond enlightenment? Please comment.

Western psychology is in its very childhood. It is little more than a century old. The concept of enlightenment belongs to Eastern psychology, which is almost ten thousand years old.

The modern Western psychology is just beginning from scratch, it is at the ABC stage. Enlightenment and beyond enlightenment are the very end of the alphabet of human endeavour, the XYZ.

Modern psychology is a misnomer because the word "psychology" originates from the word "psyche". Psyche means the soul. The exact meaning of the word "psychology" would be the science of the soul. But it is a very weird word.

Psychology denies the existence of the soul, and still goes on calling itself "psychology". It accepts only the physical body and its by-product, the mind. As the physical body dies, the mind also dies; there is no rebirth, there is no reincarnation. Life is not an eternal principle, but just a by-product of certain physical material things put together.

You have to understand the word "by-product". Even the idea of a by-product is not very original. In India, there has been a school of materialists, at least five thousand years old, called Charvakas. They describe mind as a by-product of the body. Their example is very fitting. Remember, it is a five-thousand-year-old example. We can find contemporary parallels to it.

In India people chew betel leaves, *pan*. *Pan* consists of four or five things – the betel leaf and three or four things more. You can eat them separately and they will not give the colour red to your lips; but if you eat them together they will create the colour red as a by-product. That red colour has no existence of its own, it is a by-product.

In a more contemporary example, look at a watch working.

I have heard that Mulla Nasruddin, when he retired, was presented with a gold pocket watch by his friends. It was automatic, and from the very beginning he was surprised; he thought it was a miracle that it went on and on without even winding it. But after three or four days it stopped. He was very much surprised: what had happened?

When it stopped he opened it up and found a small dead ant inside.

He said, "Now I know the secret! This ant is the driver, and now he's dead how can the watch continue? But those idiots should have told me that there is a driver! – it needs food, it needs water. And sometimes you even have to change drivers to give them a break!"

When a watch is running, and if it is automatic, what makes it tick? Is there some immaterial entity like a soul? Open the watch and take the parts apart, and you will not find any soul. That's what the Charvakas said five thousand years ago: that if there is a soul, when you cut a man open you should find it. Or when soldiers are cut open in the war, so many souls would be flying upwards. Or, when a death happens naturally in your house, the soul must leave the body.

Charvakas were very stubborn materialists. In five thousand years, materialism has not gone even a step further. They weighed a dying person, and when he was dead they weighed him again and the weight was the same – it proves that nothing left the body. Then what was ticking in the body? It was something, but just a by-product of the constituents of the body.

The materialists of all ages – Epicurus in Greece, Marx and Engels in Germany and England – continued to repeat the same idea that consciousness is a by-product. And modern psychology has accepted it as their basic foundation. They say there is no soul in man; man is only a body.

Joseph Stalin was able to kill almost one million Russians after the revolution. Anybody who was unwilling to give up his rights to his property was killed mercilessly. The whole family of the czar which had ruled for hundreds of years – one of the oldest empires in the world, and one of the biggest – 19 persons in that family were killed so mercilessly that they did not even leave a six-month-old baby, they killed that baby too. Killing was easy because of the materialist philosophy – nothing is killed, it is almost like breaking a chair. Otherwise it would be difficult for any man to kill a million people and not feel any prick in his conscience. But the philosophy was supportive of all these murders – because nothing is murdered, only the physical body. There is no consciousness which is separate from the body.

Modern psychology is still behaving stupidly because it is still clinging to the five-thousand-year-old primitive idea of Charvakas that consciousness is a by-product. Hence, all that modern psychology can do is a mechanical job.

Your car is broken down. You go to the workshop and a mechanic fixes it. The psychologist is a mechanic, no different from a plumber. He simply fixes nuts and bolts in your mind which get loose once in a while; he tightens them here and there . . . somewhere they are too tight, somewhere they are loose. But it is a question of nuts and bolts.

The question of enlightenment does not arise for the modern psychologist because enlightenment is based on the experience that mind is not your whole reality.

Beyond mind there is your consciousness, and going beyond mind is what enlightenment is all about. At the moment you cross the borders of the mind, there is enlightenment, a world of tremendous light, awareness, fulfilment, rejoicings.

But there is a possibility to go even beyond that – because that is your individual consciousness. If you can go beyond it, you enter into the cosmic consciousness.

We are living in the ocean of cosmic consciousness, just as a fish lives in the ocean and is not aware of the ocean. Because it is born in the ocean, it lives in the ocean, it dies in the ocean, the fish knows only the ocean. If a fisherman pulls it out of the ocean, throws it in the sand on the beach, then for the first time it becomes aware that something had been surrounding it, nursing it, and giving it life – and that without it, it cannot remain alive.

It is easy to give a fish the experience of being out of the ocean. It is very difficult to give man the experience of being out of the cosmic consciousness. Because the cosmic consciousness is everywhere – there is no beach, there are no boundaries to the cosmic consciousness. So wherever you are, you are always in an invisible ocean of consciousness.

Modern psychology stops at the mind.

Mind is only an instrument, and it is an instrument of the physical body – so they are not wrong in saying that it is a by-product. But mind is not all. Mind is only a bio-computer, and the day is not far away when the function of the mind will be almost taken over by computers. Any information about any subject will be immediately available, so there is no need to remember it, there is no need to read it, there is no need to study it. Your mind is going to lose its job very soon.

But the psychologist is concerned only with the mind. And there are people called behaviorists who say that man is only a physical organism. These people don't even accept the existence of the mind, but only the behavior of your body. For them, if somebody's mind is behaving in an abnormal way then medicine is needed, not psychoanalysis. Then the person has to be hospitalized; he is suffering from a sickness just like any other sickness.

At least the psychologists in the West have taken the first step beyond the body – not a very big step, very small, negligible, but still a step accepting that there is something like mind, and that although it is a by-product it functions on its own as long as the body is alive. So now it is a great profession: psychologists, psychoanalysts, psychotherapists; they are all fixing people's minds – because everybody's mind is in trouble.

There are only two kinds of people in the world: normally mad, and abnormally mad. Normally mad means you are mad, but not beyond limits. You are mad just like everybody else.

You can see these normally mad people watching a football match. Now can a sane person watch a football match? They need some nuts and bolts . . . Because with a few idiots on this side and a few idiots on that side throwing a ball, and millions of idiots so excited in the stadium and at their television sets, glued to their chairs for six hours so they cannot move . . . as if something immensely valuable is happening because a

114

ball is being thrown from this side to that side. And millions more, who are not so fortunate to be able to see, keep a radio at their ears, at least listening to the commentary.

You call this world sane?

There are boxing matches: people are hitting each other, and millions of people are so excited. In California, the University of California has discovered through their research that whenever a boxing match happens in California the crime rate immediately rises by 13 per cent; and it remains 13 per cent higher for seven to ten days afterwards – rape, murder, suicide. Boxing is simply our animal heritage. The one who gets excited in you is the animal – it is not you. You also want to kill somebody – many times you have thought of killing somebody – but you are not ready to take the consequences.

In a boxing match there is a psychological consolation; you get identified. Every boxer has his own fans. Those fans are identified with him. If he hits the opponent and the opponent's nose is dripping blood, they are rejoicing. What they have not been able to do, somebody else is doing on their behalf.

In any world that is sane, boxing would be a crime. It is a game, but all your games seem to be primitive . . . nothing of intelligence, nothing of humanity.

These normally mad people are always just on the boundary line. At any time they can slip. A small accident – the wife dies or goes away with somebody else – and you forget the normal boundary, you cross it. Then you are declared mad, insane, and immediately you have to be taken to the psychiatrist or the psychoanalyst.

And what is his function? His profession is among the highest-paid professions in the world. Naturally he makes people normal again, he pulls them back, he keeps them from going further away from the normal line. His whole expertise is how to put you back and make you normally mad.

Naturally the people who are functioning as psychologists, psychoanalysts, psychotherapists are in danger because they are constantly dealing with mad people. More psychologists go mad than any other profession – the number is twice as great. More psychologists commit suicide than any other profession – the number again is twice as great. And once in a while every psychologist goes to another psychologist to put himself back into the normal world, because he is slipping out.

One would expect that at least the psychologist should be a sane person; he is trying to help other insane people. But this is not the case. They behave more insanely than anybody else, for the simple reason that from morning till night they are constantly coming in contact with all kinds of weird, strange people with weird ideas. If you come across such people the whole day long, in the night you will dream of the same people. Naturally, psychologists don't live a very sane life.

And they cannot live a sane life until and unless they accept that there is something beyond mind.

The beyond is the rest, the shelter. Mind is a continuous chattering, it is 24 hours chattering. Only beyond mind is peace and silence. In that peace and silence sanity is born.

Enlightenment is the ultimate peak of sanity – when one becomes perfectly sane, has come to a point where silence, serenity, consciousness are 24 hours his, waking or sleeping. There runs a current of tranquillity, blissfulness, benediction, which is a nourishment, food from the beyond.

Eastern psychology accepts mind as the lowest part of human consciousness – dismal and dark. You have to go beyond it.

And enlightenment is not the end, because it is only individual consciousness. Individuality is still like two banks of a river. The moment the river moves into the ocean, all banks disappear, all boundaries are annihilated. You have gone beyond enlightenment.

Modern psychology has to learn much from the Eastern experiment. It knows nothing. All that modern psychology is doing is analysing dreams, fixing people to somehow carry on their normal business and repressing their abnormalities. But it brings no transformation.

Even the founders of modern psychology – Freud or Jung or Adler or Assagioli – are not people you can put in the category of Gautam Buddha, Lao Tzu, Chuang Tzu. You cannot put these people with the seers of the Upanishads, with Kabir and Nanak and Farid. These are the sanest people humanity has produced, and they have not bothered about dreams, nor have they gone through psychoanalysis for years together.

It is such a strange phenomenon: in the whole world there is not a single person who has completed psychoanalysis – because it goes on and on, 10 years, 12 years. There are people who have been in psychoanalysis for 20 years, wasting hundreds of thousands of dollars.

In fact, just as some people talk about diamonds and emeralds and rubies, others say, "How long have you been in psychoanalysis? I have been in it for 13 years!" It is a criterion of wealth; it shows you can afford to pay hundreds of thousands of dollars.

The poor psychoanalyst has to listen to all kinds of garbage. No wonder that they start going mad, they start committing suicide, they jump from the window of a 30-storey building! Just listen to a woman's dreams for 20 years . . . It is a great relief for the husband, he is perfectly happy that she throws all her garbage and tantrums and everything on the psychoanalyst – it is not too costly, he can manage to pay – but for the poor psychoanalyst, 20 years of listening to one woman and her stupid dreams? If one day he suddenly jumps out of the window, you cannot condemn him – he needs everybody's sympathy.

But it is big business. Modern psychology will not accept meditation because meditation will destroy their business.

A man of meditation needs no psychoanalysis. The deeper his meditation goes, the saner he becomes and the further beyond the mind is his flight. Meditation is the greatest danger for psychoanalysis, for psychologists. They have to insist that there is nothing beyond mind because if there is something beyond mind, then their whole business can flop.

The East has to assert itself, to show that what they are doing is simply foolish.

In a Zen monastery in Japan the same kind of psychological case is treated within three weeks; in the West he would not be treated in 12 years. And in the Zen monastery in those three weeks there is no psychoanalysis. You will be surprised: nothing is done; the person is put in an isolated place – a beautiful garden with a pond. In time food will be provided, in time tea will be sent; but nobody will talk with him, he has to remain silent. You can see the difference.

In psychoanalysis a person has to talk about his dreams continuously, for years, an hour every time he visits the therapist, two or three sessions a week – as much as he can afford. And here in a Zen monastery they simply put the man in a beautiful, comfortable place. There are musical instruments available, painting material is available, or if there is anything special he wants to do, that is made available; but it has to be something to *do* – not talking. And for three weeks nobody will talk to him.

During the three weeks, people paint, people play music, people dance, people work in the garden, and after three weeks they are perfectly normal, they are ready to go back home.

What has happened? If you ask the Zen master, he would say, "Nothing; these people were working too hard, and their mind got wound up too much. They needed unwinding. So just three weeks' rest and their mind was unwound. They needed physical work so that the whole energy goes into the body, not in the mind." And these people certainly become interested . . . without doing anything, all the strange and weird things that they had been thinking had disappeared. This is a simple way for sick people to unwind the overloaded mind.

For those who are healthy – not sick people – the way is meditation. There are different methods for different types. And thousands of people have achieved such luminosity, such glory, such godliness, that all the psychologists of the world should be ashamed. They have not been able to produce a single person. Even their founders are just very ordinary – worse than ordinary.

Sigmund Freud was so afraid of death that even the word "death" was prohibited. In his presence nobody should mention the word "death" because just hearing the word he would fall into a fit, he would go unconscious. These are the founders of modern psychology; they are going to give humanity sanity!

And on the other hand . . . A Zen monk, just before dying, said to his disciples: "Listen, I have always lived in my own way. I am an independent person and I want to die in my own way also. When I am dead I will not be here, so I will give you the instructions to be followed."

Just as in India, it happens in exactly the same way in Japan too; before he is taken to the funeral, the person's clothes are changed, he is given a bath and new clothes are put on him. This monk said, "I have taken the bath myself, I have changed my clothes, you can see. So when I am dead, there is no need for any bath or changing of clothes. And these are the orders from your master, so remember: at least a dying man's wishes should not be denied – and I am not asking much."

His disciples said, "We will do as you say. There is nothing much in it."

He died, and thousands of disciples were there. When his body was put on the funeral pyre, they all started laughing and giggling – he had hidden firecrackers inside his clothes. He had made it into a celebration, a fireworks show, just to make everybody laugh – because that was his basic teaching, that life should be a dance, a joy, and death should be a celebration. Even after death he managed it so that nobody should stand around him with a long face, so that everybody was laughing. Even the strangers who had come started laughing; they had never seen such a scene.

These are the people who have understood life and death. They can make death a joke.

Not Sigmund Freud, for whom the word "death" becomes a fit.

And the same is the case with other great psychologists. Jung wanted to go to Egypt to see the old mummies of kings and queens, dead bodies preserved for three thousand years. But he was very much afraid of death and dead bodies. He was a disciple of Freud. He booked the ticket 12 times, and each time he would find some excuse: "I am feeling feverish", or, "Some urgent work has come."

And he knew. He wrote in his diary: "I knew it was all an excuse. I was avoiding going to Egypt, but the more I avoided it the more I was attracted – as if I had to go, it was a challenge to my manliness. Am I such a coward? So I would book again, and I would gather courage, and I would try to convince myself that there is nothing to be worried about – they are dead bodies, they cannot do anything to you. And so many people go to see them. They are there in the museums. Thousands of people see them every day. Why are you afraid?" – but arguments won't do.

Finally, the twelfth time he booked, he managed to get to the airport, but when the plane came on the airstrip all his courage, arguments and everything disappeared. He said, "I am feeling very sick and nauseous. I want to go back home. Cancel the trip." And after that, he never dared book again; 12 times was enough. He never managed to reach Egypt – which was only a few hours' flight.

He came to India, and he went to all the universities of India. He was in the country for three months, but he would not go to one man, to whom he needed to go. He would not go to Raman Maharshi. And in every university it was suggested that he was wasting his time: "You have come to understand the Eastern approach, but our faculty members are all educated in a Western way. You are just wasting your time. We may have been educated in the West or in the East, but in both cases our education is Western; we know nothing of the East. But by chance there is a man – he knows nothing of psychology, he is absolutely uneducated, but he represents the East. This man has experienced the ultimate flights of meditation. You just go and sit by his side."

Jung went up to Madras, but he would not go to see Raman Maharshi. It was only a two-hour journey from Madras, but he would not go. And he had come to India to understand what the Eastern attitude to psychology was.

Western psychology – which is the contemporary psychology – is very childish.

The East has a ten-thousand-year-old enquiry into human consciousness. It has touched every nook and corner of human being, within and without, as individual and as universal.

But it is unfortunate that even the Eastern psychologists and professors of psychology have no idea about the Eastern approach. They are just parrots repeating Western psychology second-hand. That too is not their own original contribution. Sometimes even parrots are better and more intelligent.

I have been a professor in the university, and I have been in constant conflict with the professors: "You are parrots and you are agents of the West without your knowing. You are corrupting the Eastern mind because you don't know what you are doing. You are not even aware of what the East has already discovered. You are just carbon copies carrying certificates from Western universities."

I have often told a story in the universities.

A bishop was looking for a parrot. His own parrot had died. It had been a very religious parrot – religious in the sense that it was able to repeat the Sermon on the Mount accurately, word for word. And whoever heard it was simply amazed. The parrot had died and the bishop was missing his parrot.

So he went to a very big pet shop, and he looked around. There were many parrots there with many qualities. But he said, "No, my parrot was almost a saint; I want a very religious parrot."

The pet-shop owner said, "I have a special parrot – but the price may be too much. He is no ordinary saint, he is a very special saint. Come inside with me. I keep my special parrots in my house behind the shop, not in the shop itself.

There in a golden cage was a beautiful parrot.

The pet-shop owner said, "This is the religious parrot. You have talked so much about your parrot, but this parrot is unique – you will forget all about the other one. Come close and see: on its right leg there is a small thread; if you pull that thread, it will repeat the Sermon on the Mount. There is also a small thread on its left leg; if you pull that, it will repeat the Song of Solomon. So if you have a Jew for a guest, you can make the parrot repeat the Song of Solomon from the Old Testament; if you have a Christian guest, then the Sermon on the Mount from the New Testament."

The bishop said, "Great; this is really great. And what will happen if I pull both threads together?"

Before the owner could say anything, the parrot said, "Never do that, you idiot. I will fall on my ass!"

Even parrots have some intelligence.

Sooner or later psychology has to enquire into the states created by meditation, into spaces which are beyond mind. And unless it dares to penetrate the innermost core of human beings, it will not become a science. Right now its name is wrong; it has to prove that it is psychology – the science of the soul.

Limitations of the Scientific Approach

All the psychologies in the West are concerned with figuring out the functioning of the mind – how it works, why it sometimes works right and sometimes wrong. They have accepted one basic hypothesis that is not true: the hypothesis that you are no more than mind, that you are a body-mind. Naturally, physiology looks into your body and its functioning and psychology looks into your mind and its functioning.

The first point to be noted is that there are those who have come to know a different space in themselves that cannot be confined by the mind and that cannot be defined as part of the functioning of the mind. That silent space, with no thoughts, no ripples, is the foundation of the psychology of the buddhas.

The word 'psychology' is being used all over the world absolutely wrongly, but when something becomes commonplace we forget. Even the very word psychology indicates not something about the mind, but about the psyche. The root meaning of psychology is "the science of the soul". It is not the science of the mind. And if people are honest, they should change the name, because it is a wrong name and takes people on wrong paths. There exists no psychology in the world in the sense of a science of the soul.

You are, to use arbitrary terms – just to be able to understand – divided into three parts. But remember, the division is only arbitrary. You are an indivisible unit.

The body is your outer part. It is an immensely valuable instrument that existence has given to you. You have never thanked existence for your body. You are not even aware what it goes on doing for you, for 70 years, 80 years, in some places more than a hundred years. The ordinary conception that the body dies at the age of 70 is not a fact but a fiction that has become so prevalent that the body simply follows it.

It happened that before George Bernard Shaw reached the age of 90 – his friends were very puzzled – he started looking for a place outside London, where he had lived his whole life. They asked, "What is the point? You have a beautiful house, all the facilities; why are you looking for a new place to live? And you are looking in a very strange way – a few people think you have gone senile." Because he would go around to the villages, not into the towns but into the cemeteries, and he would read what was written on the gravestones. Finally he decided to live in a village where he found a gravestone where it was written that "This man died a very untimely death – he was only 112 years old."

He said to his friends, "As far as I am concerned, it is a worldwide hypnosis. Because the idea of 70 years has been insisted on for so many years, man's body simply follows it. If there is a village where a man dies at 112 and the villagers think he died 'untimely', that this was not the time for him to die . . ." Shaw lived in that village during his last years, and he completed the century.

Seventy years has become a fixed point, almost all over the world. But it is not the truth of the body. It is a corruption of the body by the mind.

Strangely enough, all the religions are against the body –
and the body is your life, the body is your communion with
existence. It is the body that breathes, it is the body that
keeps you alive, it is the body that does almost miracles. Do
you have any idea how to change a loaf of bread into blood
and sort it out into its different constituents and send those
constituents where they are needed? How much oxygen your
brain needs – have you any idea? Just in six minutes, if your
brain does not get oxygen, you will fall into a coma. Day after
day, the body continues to supply the exact amount of oxygen
to your brain.

How do you explain the process of breathing? Certainly
you are not breathing; it is the body that goes on breathing.
If *you* were breathing, you would not have been here. There
are so many worries, you could have forgotten to breathe, and
particularly in the night – either you could breathe or you
could sleep! And it is not a simple process, because the air the
body takes in consists of many elements that are dangerous
to you. The body sorts out only those elements that are
nourishing to life and it breathes out all that is dangerous to
you, particularly carbon dioxide.

The wisdom of the body has not been appreciated by any
religion of the world. Your wisest people were no wiser than
your body. Its functioning is so perfect – and its understanding
has been kept completely out of your control because your
control could have been destructive.

The first part of your life and being is your body. The body
is real, authentic, sincere. A deep respect, love and gratitude
for your body will be the fundamental of the psychology of
the buddhas, of the psychology of the awakened ones.

The second thing after the body is your mind. Mind is
simply a fiction. It has been used, in fact used too much, by all

kinds of parasites. These are the people who will teach you to be against the body and for the mind. There is a mechanism called the brain. The brain is part of the body, but the brain has no inbuilt programme. Nature is so compassionate – leaving your brain without any inbuilt programme means existence is giving you freedom. Whatever you want to make of your brain, you can make.

But what was compassionate on the part of nature has been exploited by your priests, your politicians, your so-called great men. They found a great opportunity to stuff the mind with all kinds of nonsense. Mind is a clean slate – whatever you write on the mind becomes your theology, your religion, your political ideology. And every parent, every society is so alert not to leave your brain in your own hands, they immediately start writing the Holy Koran, the Holy Bible, Bhagavad-Gita – and by the time they call you adult, able to participate in the affairs of the world, you are no longer yourself.

This is so cunning, so criminal, that I am surprised nobody has pointed it out.

No parent has the right to force a child to be a Catholic or a Hindu or a Jain. Children are born through you but they don't belong to you. You cannot be the possessors of living beings. You can love them, and if you really love them you will give them freedom to grow according to their own nature, without any coercion, without any punishment, without any effort by anybody else to impose.

The brain is perfectly right – it is the freedom given by nature to you, a space to grow. But the society, before you can grow that space, stuffs it with all kinds of nonsense. It should be clearly understood: the brain is natural; mind is what is stuffed into the brain. So the brain is not Christian, but mind can be; the brain is not Hindu, but the mind can be.

The mind is the creation of the society, not a gift of nature. The first thing the psychology of the buddhas will do is to take away this whole junk that you call mind and leave your brain silent, pure – innocent, the way you were born.

Modern psychology all around the world is analysing the brain, analysing all the thoughts that constitute your mind. In the East we have looked into the innermost parts of humanity and our understanding is that the mind needs no analysis, it is analysing junk. It needs simply to be erased. The moment the mind is erased – and the method is meditation – you are left with a body that is absolutely beautiful, and you are left with a silent brain with no noise. The moment the brain is freed from the mind, the innocence of the brain becomes aware of a new space, which we have called the soul.

Once you have found your soul, you have found your home. You have found your love, you have found your inexhaustible ecstasy, you have found that the whole existence is ready for you to dance, to rejoice, to sing – to live intensely and die blissfully. These things happen on their own accord.

The mind is the barrier between your brain, your body and your soul. You can see the difference: the psychology born in the West is concerned with the most non-essential part of you; it goes round and round analysing the mind. The psychology of the buddhas, in a single hit, will drop the mind and accept only that which existence has given to you, not whatever society you were unfortunate to be born in.

But every society is unfortunate, every religion is unfortunate. This is the greatest calamity under which humanity has lived up to now.

What is the difference between a Mohammedan and a Christian, except the mind? What is the difference between a communist and a spiritualist? – just the difference of the mind. Each has been cultivated differently.

So the first and the most basic thing is, the psychology of the buddhas has evolved methods of meditation which are really nothing but surgical methods so that the mind can be removed – it is the worst cancerous growth in you. Other than the mind, everything is absolutely beautiful. It is because only the mind is man-manufactured; everything else comes from the eternal sources of life.

The psychology of the buddhas is not a science in the sense you understand it, because science remains confined to the mind. It is more like an art. Its methods of working are arbitrary, they are not scientific.

I will give you an example to show that science is a very much lower phenomenon . . .

One morning Chuang Tzu sat up in his bed – which was strange, because he used to get up and get out of his bed. Why is he sitting and looking so sad? He was not a man of sadness.

In fact I have not found anybody else in the whole world of literature who has written such beautiful absurd stories. They don't make any sense, but they are beautiful.

He was creating a situation.

The disciples were worried; they came and they asked, "What is the matter?"

Chuang Tzu said, "I am in a very great fix: last night I slept, and I knew perfectly well that I was Chuang Tzu. But in the night I had a dream that I had become a butterfly."

The disciples laughed. He said, "Shut up! It is not a matter to laugh about; my whole life is at risk!"

They said, "Master, it was only a dream!"

He said, "First you should listen to the whole thing. Then in the morning I woke up and the idea arose in me that if

Chuang Tzu can become a butterfly in a dream, what is the guarantee that a butterfly cannot become Chuang Tzu in a dream? And now the question is, who am I? The butterfly dreaming, or . . .?"

Certainly the situation he has created is almost insoluble. Do you think there can be any rational solution to it? His question is very pertinent: if Chuang Tzu can become a butterfly in a dream, perhaps the butterfly has gone to sleep and has become Chuang Tzu. The problem is that Chuang Tzu is losing his identity. He told the disciples, "Meditate and find a solution. Unless you find a solution I am going to sit in my bed without eating, because it is a question of life and death."

They went out, they discussed it . . . "This is absolutely absurd! We have also dreamt, but this idea . . ." But the idea is such that there is no way out of it!

Then came Lieh Tzu, Chuang Tzu's chief disciple, and all the disciples asked him what to do. He said, "Don't be worried", and rather than going to Chuang Tzu, he went to the water well. They said, "Where are you going?"

He said, "You just wait. I know my master." He pulled out a bucket of water – it was a cold winter morning – and he brought the bucket of water and poured it on Chuang Tzu!

Chuang Tzu laughed and he said, "If you had not come, my life was at risk. You saved me!"

Lieh Tzu said, "Just get out of the bed, or I am going to bring another bucket of water. All that you need is to be brought out of your dream. You are still dreaming."

He said, "No, I am going to get out!"

The masters cannot create a science, because science can only be objective. At the most you can call it an art, because the art has more flexibility, more different approaches . . .

Now, what do you call Lieh Tzu's bringing a bucket of water? A scientific method? Just a clear insight, and out of that clear insight arises an arbitrary, artful but intelligent method.

In fact, Chuang Tzu was waiting for some disciple to *do* something – it was not a question to be solved by sitting and pondering over it. The question was such that somebody had to *do* something and show his clarity by his act. This was the moment Chuang Tzu declared Lieh Tzu to be his successor. All the other disciples could not understand what had happened – what kind of solution is this? The psychology of the buddhas is not a science, is not a philosophy. At the most we can call it a very flexible art. There are no fixed answers for anything.

The psychology of the buddhas cannot be a science. Science is always objective, it is about the other. It is never about your own being. It is extrovert, it is never introvert. But the man who has become awakened finds ways to shake you from your sleep, to wake you from your mind, which is your coma, which is your blindness. That's why different masters in different countries have used different methods. No method is scientific. It depends on the person who has to be operated upon. The surgery cannot be a definite science. As far as the psychology of the buddhas is concerned, it is going to be very flexible.

Yes, sometimes the master may hit you and sometimes the master may hug you. But it all depends on what kind of mind he is working on, and he is working on different kinds of minds. You don't have the same minds; otherwise the same method would have been enough.

Traditionally there are 108 methods of meditation. I have gone through all those methods – not just by reading them; I have tried every method. My search was to find what is the essential core of all those 108 methods, because there is bound to be something essential. And my experience is that the essential of all meditations is the art of witnessing.

Then I created my own methods because I had found the essential core. Those 108 methods have become, in a way, out of date. They were created by different masters for different kinds of people, to transform different minds. The contemporary mind did not yet exist; the contemporary mind needs new methods. The methods will differ only in non-essentials. The essential core, the very soul of the method, is going to be the same.

Just to Be Normal
Is Not Enough

Sigmund Freud introduced psychoanalysis into the world. It is rooted in analysing the mind. It is confined to the mind. It does not step out of the mind, not even an inch. On the contrary, it goes deeper into the mind, into the hidden layers of the mind, into the unconscious, to find out ways and means so that the mind of man can at least be normal. The goal of Freudian psychoanalysis is not very great.

The goal is to keep people normal. But normality is not enough. Just to be normal is not of any significance. It means the normal routine of life and your capacity to cope with it. It does not give you meaning, it does not give you significance. It does not give you insight into the reality of things. It does not take you beyond time, beyond death. It is at the most a helpful device for those who have gone so abnormal that they have become incapable of coping with their daily lives – they cannot live with people, they cannot work, they have become shattered. Psychotherapy provides them with a certain togetherness – not integrity, mind you, but only a certain togetherness. It binds them into a bundle. They remain fragmentary; nothing becomes crystallized in them, no soul is born. They don't become blissful, they are only less unhappy, less miserable.

Psychology helps people to accept their misery. It helps them to accept that this is all that life can give to you, so don't ask for more. In a way, it is dangerous to their inner growth, because the inner growth happens only when there is a divine discontent. When you are absolutely unsatisfied with things as they are, only then do you go in search; only then do you start rising higher, only then do you make efforts to pull yourself out of the mud.

Jung went a little further into the unconscious. He went into the collective unconscious – this is getting more and more into muddy water, and it is not going to help. Assagioli moved to the other extreme. Seeing the failure of psychoanalysis, he invented psychosynthesis . . . but it is rooted in the same idea. Instead of analysis he emphasizes synthesis.

The psychology of the buddhas, the psychological insight of the East, is neither analysis nor synthesis; it is transcendence, it is going beyond the mind. It is not work within the mind, it is work that takes you outside the mind. That's exactly the meaning of the English word "ecstasy" – to stand out.

When you are capable of standing outside of your own mind, when you are capable of creating a distance between your mind and your being, then you have taken the first step toward the psychology of the buddhas. A miracle happens: when you are standing outside of the mind all the problems of the mind disappear because mind itself disappears; it loses its grip over you.

Psychoanalysis is like pruning leaves of the tree, but new leaves will be coming up. It is not cutting off the roots. Psychosynthesis is sticking the fallen leaves back onto the tree again, gluing them back to the tree. That is not going to give them life either. They will look simply ugly; they will not be alive, they will not be green, they will not be part of the tree but glued, somehow.

The psychology of the buddhas cuts the very roots of the tree, which create all kinds of neuroses, psychoses, which create the fragmentary man, the mechanical man, the robot-like man. Psychoanalysis takes years, and still the person remains the same. It is renovating the old structure, patching up here and there, whitewashing the old house. But it is the same house; nothing has radically changed. It has not transformed the consciousness of the person.

The psychology of the buddhas does not work within the mind; it has no interest in analysing or synthesizing. It simply helps you to get out of the mind so that you can have a look from the outside. And that very look is a transformation. The moment you can look at your mind as an object, you become detached from it, you become disidentified with it; a distance is created and the roots are cut.

Why are the roots cut in this way? Because it is you who goes on feeding the mind. If you are identified you feed the mind; if you are not identified you stop feeding it. It drops of its own accord.

There is a beautiful story. I love it very much . . .

One day Buddha is passing through a forest. It is a hot summer day and he is feeling very thirsty. He says to Ananda, his chief disciple, "Ananda, you go back. Just three, four miles back we passed a small stream of water. Take my begging bowl, and bring back a little water – I am feeling very thirsty and tired."

Ananda goes back, but by the time he reaches the stream, a few bullock carts have just passed through and they have made the whole stream muddy. Dead leaves that had settled into the streambed have risen up; it is no longer possible to drink this water, it is too dirty. He comes back empty-handed, and he says, "You will have to wait a little. I will go ahead; I have heard that just two, three miles ahead there is a big river. I will bring water from there."

But Buddha insists. He says, "You go back and bring water from that same stream."

Ananda could not understand the insistence, but if the master asks him to do something the disciple has to follow. Seeing the absurdity of it – that again he will have to walk three, four miles, and he knows the water is not worth drinking – he goes.

As he is going, Buddha says, "And don't come back if the water is still dirty. If it is dirty, you simply sit on the bank silently. Don't do anything, don't get into the stream. Sit on the bank silently and watch. Sooner or later the water will be clear again, and then you can fill the bowl and come back."

Ananda goes there. Buddha is right: the water is almost clear, the leaves have started to settle again, and the mud. But the stream is not absolutely clear yet, so he sits on the bank just watching the water flow by. Slowly, slowly, it becomes crystal clear. Then he comes back dancing; then he understands why Buddha was so insistent. There was a certain message in it for him and he understood the message. He gave the water to Buddha, and he thanked him, touched his feet.

Buddha says, "What are you doing? I should thank you that you have brought water for me."

Ananda says, "Now I can understand. First I was angry; I didn't show it but I was angry because it was absurd to go back. But now I understand the message. This is what I actually needed in this moment. The same is the case with my mind – sitting on the bank of that small stream, I became aware that the same is the case with my mind. If I jump into the stream I will make it dirty again. If I jump into the mind more noise is created, more problems start coming up, surfacing. Sitting by the side of the stream I learned the technique.

"Now I will be sitting by the side of my mind too, watching it with all its dirtiness and problems and old leaves and hurts and wounds, memories, desires. Unconcerned I will sit on the bank and wait for the moment when everything is clear."

And it happens on its own, because the moment you sit on the bank of your mind you are no longer giving energy to it. This is real meditation. Meditation is the art of transcendence.

Freud talks about analysis, Assagioli about synthesis. Buddhas have always talked about meditation, awareness.

Meditation, awareness, watchfulness, witnessing – that is the uniqueness of the psychology of transcendence. No psychoanalyst is needed. You can do it on your own; in fact, you *have* to do it on your own. No guidelines are needed, it is such a simple process – simple if you do it; if you don't do it, it looks very complicated. Even the word "meditation" scares many people. They think it something very difficult, arduous. Yes, it is difficult and arduous if you don't do it . . . It is like swimming. It is very difficult if you don't know how to swim, but if you know swimming, you know it is so simple a process. Nothing can be simpler than swimming. It is not complicated at all; it is so spontaneous and so natural.

Be more aware of your mind. And in being aware of your mind you will become aware of the fact that you are not the mind, and that is the beginning of the revolution. You have started flowing higher and higher. You are no longer tethered to the mind. Mind functions like a rock and keeps you down. It keeps you within the field of gravitation. The moment you are no longer attached to the mind, you enter the buddhafield. When gravitation loses its power over you, you enter into the buddhafield, and entering the buddhafield means entering the world of levitation. You start floating upwards.

Mind goes on dragging you downwards. So it is not a question of analysing or synthesizing. It is simply a question of becoming aware. That's why in the East we have not developed any psychotherapy like Freudian or Jungian or Adlerian . . . and there are so many in the market now. We have not developed a single psychotherapy because we know psychotherapies can't heal. They may help you to accept your wounds, but they can't heal. Healing comes when you are no longer attached to the mind. When you are disconnected from the mind, unidentified, absolutely untethered, when the bondage is finished, then healing happens.

Transcendence is true therapy, and it is not only psychotherapy. It is not only a phenomenon limited to your psychology, it is far more than that. It is spiritual. It heals you in your very being.

In intensive psychotherapy the patient may either be talking or listening, that is, trying to hear from within. Only the latter is of value. A good therapist, especially if love exists, will hit on many ways of heightening this process of listening for the unexpected. Is this a form of meditation? In fact, might it be said that, ideally, both therapist and patient are meditating together?

Therapy is basically meditation and love, because without love and meditation there is no healing possible. When the therapist and the patient are not two, when the therapist is not only a therapist and when the patient is not a patient any more, but a deep I–thou relationship arises where the therapist is not trying to treat the person, when the patient is not looking at the therapist as separate from himself – in those rare moments, therapy happens. When the therapist has forgotten his knowledge, and the patient has forgotten his illness, and there is a dialogue, a dialogue of two beings, in that moment, between the two, healing happens. And if it happens, the therapist will always know that he functioned only as a vehicle for a divine force, for a divine healing. He will be as grateful for the experience as the patient. In fact, he will gain as much out of it as the patient.

When you treat a person as a patient, you treat him as if he is a machine. Just like a mechanic who is trying to change, to adjust a mechanism, trying to put it right, the therapist becomes an expert, hung up in his knowledge in the head. He is trying to help the other person as if the other person is not another person, but a machine. He may be technically expert, he may have the know-how, but he is not going to be of much help. Because this very viewpoint is destructive. This very looking at the patient and seeing him as an object creates a resistance in the patient; he feels hurt.

Have you watched? There are only a very few doctors with whom you don't feel humiliated, with whom you don't feel as if you have been treated as an object, with whom you feel a deep respect for you, with whom you feel that you are taken as a person, not as a mechanism. And it is more so when it is a question of psychotherapy. A psychotherapist needs to forget all that he knows. In the moment, he has to become a love, a flowing love. In the moment, he has to accept the humanity of the other, the subjectivity of the other. The other should not be reduced to a thing, otherwise you have closed the doors for a greater healing force to descend, from the very beginning. To be a therapist is one of the most difficult things in the world, because you have to know to help, and on the other hand, you have to forget all that you know to help. You have to know much to help, and you have to forget all of it to help. A therapist has to do a very contradictory thing, and only then does therapy happen. When love flows and the therapist listens to the patient with tremendous attention, and the patient also tries to listen to his own inner being, to his own unconscious talking to him – when this listening happens, by and by, in that deep listening there are not two persons. Maybe there are two polarities . . .

When you listen to me, healing is happening all the time. When you listen to me so attentively that you are not there – no mind, no thinking – you have become just the ears, you just listen, you absorb; and I am not here at all, so when in some rare moments you are also not there, there is healing. Suddenly you are healed. Without your knowing, you are being healed every day. Without your knowing, the healing surrounds you, the healing force surrounds you. Your wounds heal, your darkness disappears, your limitations are broken; this is a therapy.

In the East we have never had anything like a psychotherapist, because the master was more than enough. Whatsoever psychoanalysis knows today the East has known for centuries, nothing is new in it. But in the East, we never gave birth to the category of the psychoanalyst but rather the master, not the patient but the disciple.

Just look at the difference. When you come to me as a patient you bring a very ugly mind; when you come to me as a disciple you bring a beautiful mind. When I look at you as a therapist, that very look reduces you to a thing; when I look as master that very look raises you to the heights of your innermost being. In the East we have never called the master a "psychotherapist" even though he is the greatest therapist that has ever been known in the world. Just sitting by the side of Buddha, millions were healed. Wherever he moved there was healing, but healing was never talked about. It was simply happening; there was no need to talk about it. The very presence of Buddha, and a loving look from the master, and the readiness on the part of the disciple to absorb what was being given . . .

The idea of being a "patient" is ugly. The word in itself is not ugly; it comes from a very beautiful root. It comes from the same root as "patience", but it has become ugly by association. A disciple is totally different: you have come to learn something, not to be treated. The treatment happens by itself. All therapy is learning. In fact, why have you become mentally ill? Because you have learned something wrong. You have learned something so totally wrong that you are caught in it. You need somebody who can uncondition you, who can help you to unlearn it and channel your energy into a different path, that's all.

For example: one woman came to me. I have been watching her for many years; she has been coming to me for many years. The first time she came she told me that she was not interested in sex at all, but her husband was continuously after sex. She felt very bad about it; she was almost vomiting: "How to stop it? What should I do?" she asked. I talked to the husband and told him, "Just for one month, don't be interested sexually. After a month, things will be better and different." For one month he followed my suggestion. The woman came again. She said, "I am feeling very hurt, because my husband is not at all interested in me sexually." Then I told her, "Now, you have to understand what is happening. When your husband is sexually interested, you have a certain power over him. You enjoy that power, but at the same time you also feel that you are being used. Because the husband looks at you sexually, that means that he looks at you as

141

a means toward a certain satisfaction. You feel that you are being used." Almost all women feel that they are being used, and that is their problem. But if the husband stops taking an interest they forget all about being used, and they become afraid – then they start thinking that the husband is losing interest in them. Now they have no more power over him, they don't possess him. So I told the woman, "Just look at the fact: if you want to possess the husband you will have to be possessed by him. If you want to possess the husband, then you will have to be used by him."

A mind that is possessive will be possessed. To possess anything is to be possessed by it. The more you possess, the more slavery you create around yourself. Freedom comes when you unlearn possessiveness. When you unlearn possessiveness, then you are not in search of any power over anybody. Then jealousy does not arise. And when you are not trying to possess the other, you create such beauty around yourself that the other cannot look at you as a thing. You become a person – glorified, vibrant, illuminated – you become a light unto yourself; nobody can possess you. Whosoever comes near you will feel the tremendous beauty, and will not be able to think in terms of your being a thing.

Now every woman suffers, because in the first place she wants to possess; when she wants to possess, she is possessed; when she is possessed she feels, "I am being used." If she is not being used, then she feels that power is disappearing. So a woman always remains in a suffering, and it is the same with men.

To look deeply into a problem is to be healed, because the very look shows you that you have learned some wrong trick. Unlearn . . . there is healing. People are mentally ill because they have been conditioned wrongly. Everybody has been conditioned to be competitive and everybody has been taught to be silent and peaceful. This is stupid; you cannot be both. Either you are competitive, then you remain tense; or you are silent and peace loving, then you cannot be competitive.

You have been taught dichotomies. You have been told to move in two directions together, and you have learned it. You have been taught to be humble, and you have been continuously taught to be egoistic.

If your son is first in his class at university, you feel very happy. You give a party for his friends, and you go on telling your son that he is a great man; he is first in his class, he is being awarded a gold medal. Now this is an ego trip, as all medals are. And at the same time, you go on teaching him to be humble. Now you are creating a difficulty: if he becomes humble he will not be competitive; if he becomes competitive, he cannot be humble. If he wants to attain all the gold medals that this life can give, then he cannot be humble. Then all his humbleness will be hypocrisy. One has to see. Now this man will be in trouble: continuously he will try to be humble, and continuously he will try to succeed in life. If he succeeds, he will never enjoy the success, because he will have become arrogant and egoistic, and he had an ideal of being humble and egoless. If he becomes humble and egoless he will not feel happy, because he has that ideal to succeed in the world, to show to the world the mettle that he is made of.

The society goes on being contradictory, inconsistent, and goes on teaching you things that are absolutely wrong. Then illness happens; then there is psychic turmoil within you, conflict within you. Then you come to a point where everything is in disorder, topsy-turvy. You can either go to a master, or you can go to a psychotherapist. If you go to a master you go as a disciple, to learn. You have learned something wrong;

it has to be unlearned and something new has to be learned. When you go as a disciple you don't feel humiliated, you feel happy about it. But if you go as a mental case, if you go as a patient, you feel embarrassed. Going to a psychotherapist, you want to hide the facts – "People should not know about this, because it means that my mind is not functioning well." Going to the psychotherapist, you would like to hide it. A psychotherapist is an expert: he himself has problems, almost the same as you have; he may be of some help to you, but he has not been of much use to himself.

But a master has no problems. He can help you tremendously because he can see you through and through. You become transparent before him. A psychotherapist is a professional: even if he takes care of you, shows a certain love toward you, affection, it is a professional gesture. A master is not professionally related to you. The relationship is totally different; it is heart to heart.

There are so many psychotherapies, but nothing is proving to be helpful. Patients go from one psychoanalyst to another, from one therapy to another. Their whole lives they are moving from one door to another. Masters are needed, realized people are needed who have attained to love. But even in ordinary psychotherapy, if for some moments it happens that the patient is no longer a patient and the therapist is no longer a therapist – a certain love, a certain humanity; they have forgotten their professional relationship, and love flows – healing immediately happens.

Healing is a function of love. Love is the greatest therapy, and the world needs therapists because the world lacks love. If people were loving – if parents were loving, if teachers and professors were loving, if the society had a loving climate – there would be no need.

Everybody is born to remain healthy and happy. Everybody is seeking health and happiness, but somewhere something is missing and everybody becomes miserable. Misery should be an exception; it has become the rule. Happiness should be the rule; it has become an exception. I would like a world where buddhas are born but where nobody remembers them because they are the rule. Now Buddha is remembered, Christ is remembered, Lao Tzu is remembered, because they are exceptions. Otherwise, who would bother about them? If there were a buddha in every house, and if there were buddhas all over the marketplace and you could meet Lao Tzu anywhere, who would bother? Then that would be the simple rule. It should be so.

Lao Tzu says, "When the world was really moral there was no possibility of becoming a saint." When the world was really religious there was no need for religions. People were simply religious; religions were not needed. When there was order, a discipline, a natural order and discipline, the words "order" and "discipline" didn't exist. The idea of order comes in only when there is disorder. People start talking about discipline where there is no discipline, and people talk about healing when illness is there. People talk about love when love is missing. But basically, therapy is a function of love.

If you are a therapist, never look at the patient as a patient. Look at him as if he has come to learn something – a disciple. Help him, but not as an expert; help him like a human being, and there will be much healing. There will be less therapy and more healing. Otherwise, therapy continues for years and years on end, and the result is almost nil. Or, sometimes, the result is even harmful.

I have heard about one man who had a very curious habit: whenever he was in the pub he would drink wine and always leave a little part in the glass and throw it all around, over people. He was beaten many times. Then the owner of the pub suggested, "Why don't you go to a psychoanalyst? You need therapy because you have been beaten and you have been thrown out of the pub, but again you come and again you do the same. Something seems to be wrong. You are obsessed."

So the man went, and after three months he came back. He was looking better. The pub owner asked, "Have you been to some psychoanalyst? Because for three months you have disappeared."

The man said, "Yes, and it helped me tremendously."

"Are you cured?" the owner asked.

He said, "Perfectly cured." But then he did the same thing again!

The owner said, "What type of treatment is this? You are doing the same thing!"

The man said, "But I am completely changed. Before, I used to do it and feel guilty. I don't feel guilt any more. The psycho-analyst helped me, cured me of the guilt. I used to feel embarrassed, now I don't bother about what other people think."

This has happened: psychoanalysis has helped many people just to feel that nothing matters. It has not given a deeper responsibility, it has only taken away the feeling of guilt. The feeling of guilt is bad; it has to be taken away. But it should be taken away in such a manner that the person unlearns the idea of guilt but learns the idea of responsibility. Guilt is bad, guilt is very dangerous, it destroys you. It is like a wound. But to feel responsible is very, very essential – it gives you soul, it gives you an integration. And unless you feel responsible you are not a healthy person. A healthy person is always aware that whatsoever he is doing, he is responsible. The very idea of responsibility will give you a freedom, a dignity. An authentic being will come out of it. You will become more present, you will be more here and now.

The idea of guilt is a false coin. It looks like responsibility; it is not. Guilt makes you depressed. Responsibility will give you an intensity, a sharpness of awareness. You will have more integration in you, you will feel more together.

And if you love people, you will be loved. If you heal people, if you become a vehicle of healing force and energy, you will be healed. And always remember that while healing a person you are part of the process; you are also being healed. While teaching a person, you are also being taught. The best way in the world to learn anything is to teach it. But remember that the master is also a disciple. He continuously goes on learning. Each disciple is a new lesson, and to work with each patient, or disciple, is to open a new book, a new life.

Great are the rewards of love. Create a climate around yourself so that the patient comes to learn, to unlearn, to be transformed. He is not to be taken as a "case" but as a helpless human being, as helpless as you are. Don't look down from a tower, "holier than thou", higher than the other, more knowledgeable than the other. Don't look at the other person in that way; that gaze is violent and love becomes impossible. Look as a human being, as helpless as the other – in the same boat, in the same plight. You will be helpful, and much healing will happen through you.

I have heard an anecdote about Harvard's famed professor, Charles T. Copeland. He was once asked by a student, "Is there anything I can do to learn the art of conversation?"

"Yes, there is one thing," said Copeland; "if you listen I will tell you."

For several minutes there was silence, then the student said, "I am listening, professor."

"You see," said Copeland, "you are learning already."

Listening is learning, because when you listen silently the whole existence starts speaking to you. When you are absolutely silent, that is the greatest moment to learn.

Life reveals its secrets when you are silent.

So, whether helping a disciple, a fellow traveller, a friend, or trying to heal a patient, be a great listener. Listen so passionately, so attentively that the other becomes, by and by, capable of revealing his most secret depths to you – depths that he has not revealed to anybody because nobody was ready to listen; depths that he has not revealed to himself because he was also not ready to listen; depths that have remained always in the dark. Listen so tremendously that the very milieu of your listening brings out all that is hidden in the patient, in the disciple. He will be surprised that he is saying things to you; he never knew that those things existed in him. Through your listening you will make him aware of his own unconscious, and that is a healing thing. Once the unconscious becomes the conscious, many things disappear. All that is rubbish disappears and all that is significant deepens.

But how can you teach listening? – by being a great listener. While you are listening to a patient or a friend, don't become bored. If you are bored, please tell the person that this is not the right moment: "Some other moment; I am not in a mood to listen." Never listen to anybody when you are feeling bored, because your boredom creates a climate in which the other immediately feels that he is rejected. Your boredom goes on saying to him, "What you are saying is all rubbish. Stop, shut up." Whether you say it or not doesn't matter. Your whole being is saying, "Shut up! Be finished with it."

Because of this, Freud used to use a certain method. The method was to hide himself from the patient. The patient would lie on a couch and Freud would sit just behind him. The patient would not be able to see what Freud was thinking about, whether he was listening or not. Freud would sit at the back, and the patient would talk a monologue to himself. Freudian analysis takes many years: three, four, five, even ten years. There are even patients who have been in analysis for 20 years, and nothing has happened. It is inhuman. Face the patient; look eye to eye, don't hide like a ghost. Be human, be open, and listen.

Freud taught his disciples never to touch the patient. That is absolutely wrong, because then you become inhuman. There are moments when just holding the hand of the patient will do much, much more than all analysis can do. But Freud was very afraid that there was a possibility that intimacy might start between the doctor and the patient. The doctor should remain far away and aloof; he should not come down to the human world. Freud was very afraid, it seems, of his own humanity. He was very much afraid of his own mind. He could not allow intimacy; a very deep fear, a very deep complex must have existed in him. People who are afraid of relationship are afraid of themselves, because in relationship they are revealed, in relationship they are mirrored. Freud was a puritan.

There is no need to be so far away, otherwise healing will not happen. Come closer. The patient has to be taken in deep intimacy, so that he can reveal, so that he can bring his whole heart to you.

And respond! Don't listen like a marble statue – respond. Sometimes laugh with the person, sometimes weep and cry – respond, because when you respond, the relationship, the moment, becomes alive. If you don't respond, the whole thing goes on like a stale, dead thing. Respond; make the whole thing alive, and much is possible. Much more is possible than through just analysing, diagnosing. Freud's psychoanalysis remained a head trip. The real therapy has to be total.

Consciousness, Unconsciousness and Wholeness

One day a woman came to Mulla Nasruddin's school with her small child, her son. The woman asked Mulla to frighten the boy. He had become unruly and he would not listen to anyone. He needed to be frightened by some big authority. Of course, Mulla was a big authority in his village. He assumed a very frightening posture. His eyes were bulging, all fiery, and he began to jump. The lady felt, "Now it is impossible to stop the Mulla – he may even kill the boy."

The woman fainted, the boy escaped, and Mulla became so frightened of himself he had to run out of the school. He waited outside and the woman came back. Then he entered, slowly, silently, seriously. The woman said, "Mulla, it is strange! I never asked you to frighten *me*."

Mulla said, "You do not see the real fact. It was not only you who was frightened; I myself was frightened of myself. When fear takes over, it destroys all. To start it is easy, but to control it is difficult. So I was the master when I started, but soon fear took over and it was the master and I was the slave; I could not do anything. And, moreover, fear has no favourites. When it strikes, it strikes all."

This is a beautiful parable, one which shows a deep insight into the human mind. You are conscious in everything just in the beginning, and then the unconscious takes over. The unconscious takes charge and the unconscious becomes the master. You can start your anger, but you can never end it. Rather, the anger ends you. You can start anything, but sooner or later the unconscious takes charge; you are relieved of your duty. So only the beginning is in your hands, never the end, and you are not the master of the consequences that follow.

This is natural because only a very small fragment of the mind is aware. It works just like a starter in your car. It starts and then it is of no use; then the motor takes it over. It is needed only to start; without it, it is difficult to start. But do not go on thinking that because you start a certain thing you are the master of it. This is the secret of this parable. Because you started, you begin to feel that you are the master. Because you started, you think you could have stopped.

You may not have started, that is another thing, but once started soon the voluntary becomes the non-voluntary and the conscious becomes unconscious, because the conscious is just the upper layer, just the surface of the mind, and nearly the whole mind is unconscious. You start, and the unconscious begins to move and work.

So Mulla said, "I am not responsible for what has happened, I am not responsible! I am responsible only for starting, and it is you who told me to start. I started to frighten the boy, then the boy was frightened, then you fainted, then I was frightened, and then everything was a mess."

Everything is a mess in our lives also, with the conscious starting and the unconscious taking over every time. If you do not feel it, if you do not realize how this mechanism works, you will always be a slave. And the slavery becomes more acceptable if you go on thinking that you are the master. It is difficult to be a slave knowingly, knowing that you are a slave. It is easy to be a slave when you go on deceiving yourself that you are the master – of your love, your anger, your greed, your jealousy, your violence, your cruelty; even your sympathy and your compassion.

I say "your", but it is yours only in the beginning. Just for a moment, just the spark is yours. Then the mechanism has started, and your whole mechanism is unconscious.

Why is this so? Why this conflict between the conscious and the unconscious? And there is a conflict. You cannot predict even about yourself. Even you, your acts, are unpredictable to you, because you do not know what is going to happen, you do not know what you are going to do. You are not even aware of what you are going to do the next moment because the doer is deep in darkness. You are not the doer. You are only a starting point. Unless your whole mechanism becomes conscious, you will be a problem to yourself and a hell. There will be nothing but misery.

One can become whole in only two ways. The first is that you can lose the fragmentary consciousness, throw out this fragment of the mind which has become conscious, throw it into the dark unconscious, dissolve it, and you are whole. But then you are just like an animal, and that is impossible. Whatever you may do, it is not possible. It is conceivable, but not possible. You will be thrown forward again and again. That small part of you that has become conscious cannot become unconscious again. It is like an egg that has become a hen. Now the hen cannot move back to be an egg again. A seed that has sprouted has begun the journey to be a tree. Now it cannot go back; it cannot regress and become a seed. A child that has come out of the womb cannot now go back, no matter how pleasant the womb may be.

153

There is no going backwards. Life always moves into the future, never into the past.

Only man can think of the past. That is why I say it is conceivable, but it cannot be actualized. You can imagine, you can think to go back, you can believe in it, you can try to go back, but you cannot go. That is an impossibility. One has to move forward. And moving forward is the second way to become whole.

Knowingly or unknowingly, one is moving every moment. If you move knowingly, then the speed is accelerated. If you move knowingly, then you do not waste energy and time. Then the thing can happen even in one life which will not happen in a million lives of you just moving unknowingly, because if you move unknowingly you move in a circle. Every day you repeat the same, in every life you again repeat the same, and life becomes just a habit, a mechanical habit, a repetition.

You can break the repetitive habit if you move knowingly. Then there is a breakthrough. So the first thing is to be aware that your awareness is so small that it works only as a starter. Unless you have more awareness than unawareness, more consciousness than unconsciousness, the balance will not change.

What are the hindrances? Why is this the situation? Why is this the fact? Why this conflict between conscious and unconscious? It is natural. Whatever is, is natural. Man has evolved through millions of years. This evolution has created you, your body, your mechanism. The evolution has been a long struggle – millions and millions of experiences of failures, of successes. Your body has learned much; your body has been continuously learning things. Your body knows much, and its knowledge is fixed. It goes on repeating its own ways of behaving. Even if the situation has changed, the body remains the same. For example, when you feel anger, you feel it in the same way as any primitive man, you feel it in the same way as any animal, you feel it in the same way as any child. And this is the mechanism: when you feel anger your body has a fixed habit, a ritual, a routine work to do.

The moment your mind says "anger" you have glands that begin to release chemicals into the blood. Adrenalin is released into the blood. It is a necessity because in anger you will have to strike or else you may be struck by your opponent. You will need more blood circulation, and this chemical will help more circulation to be there. You may need to fight or you may need to escape from a situation, to run away. In both cases, this chemical will help. So when some animal is angry, the body becomes ready to fight or to take flight. And these are the two alternatives: if the animal feels that he is stronger than the opponent, he will fight; if he feels that he is not the stronger one, he will escape. The mechanism works very smoothly.

But for man the situation has become totally different. When you feel anger, you may not even express it. That is impossible for the animal, but for you it depends on the situation. If it is anger against your servants, then you may express it. If it is against your boss, then you may not express it. Not only that: you may even laugh or smile; you may even persuade your boss to think not only that you are not angry, but that you are happy. Now you are confusing the whole mechanism of the body. The body is ready to fight, and you are smiling. You are creating a mess in the body. The body cannot understand what you are doing. Are you mad? It is ready to do one of two things, which are natural: to fight or escape.

This smiling is something new. This deception is something new. The body has no mechanism for it, so you have to force the smile without the chemical flowing that helps you to smile, that helps you to laugh. Right now in this situation of anger you have no chemicals to laugh. You have to force a smile, a false smile, and the body has released chemicals into the blood to fight. Now what will the blood do? The body has a language that it understands very well, but you are behaving in an insane way. Now a gap is created between you and your body. The bodily mechanism is unconscious, it is involuntary. Your volition, your conscious intention, is not needed because conscious intention takes time and there are situations in which no time can be lost.

A tiger has attacked you – now there is no time for meditation. You cannot contemplate what to do. You have to do something without the mind. If the mind comes in you are lost. You cannot think; you cannot say to the tiger, "Wait! Let me think about it – about what to do." You have to act immediately, without any consciousness.

The body has a mechanism. The tiger is there, the mind just knows the tiger is there, and the body mechanism begins to work. That working is not dependent on the mind because mind is a very slow worker, very inefficient. It cannot be relied upon in emergency situations, so the body begins to work. You are frightened. You will run away; you will escape.

But the same thing happens when you are standing on a platform to address a big audience. There is no tiger, but you are frightened by the great gathering. Fear takes shape; the body is informed. The information that you are in fear is automatic, and the body begins to release chemicals – the same chemicals it will release when a tiger attacks you. There is no tiger, there is really no one who is attacking you, but in your mind the audience seems to represent an attack. Everyone there is aggressive, it seems, and that is why you have become afraid. Now the body is ready to fight or to take flight, but both the alternatives are closed. You have to stand there and speak!

Now your body begins to perspire, even on a cold night. Why? Because the body is ready to run or to fight. The blood is circulating more, heat is created, and you are standing there. So you begin to perspire, and then a subtle trembling takes over. Your whole body begins to tremble.

It is just the same as if you start a car and press both the accelerator and the brake simultaneously. The engine will be heated, racing, and you are braking at the same time. The whole body of the car will tremble. The same happens when you are standing on a platform. You feel fear, and the body is ready to run. The accelerator is pushed, but you cannot run – you have to address the gathering. You are a leader, or some such thing; you cannot run. You have to face it, and you have to be there standing on the platform. You have to take the floor.

Now you are doing two things simultaneously that are very contradictory. You are stepping on the accelerator and pressing the brake also. You do not run, but the body is ready to run. You begin to tremble and heat is created. Now your body wonders, "What are you doing?" The body cannot understand you; a gap is created. The unconscious is doing one thing and the conscious goes on doing something else. You are divided.

This gap has to be understood deeply.

In your every act this gap is there. You are looking at a film, an erotic film, and your sexuality is aroused. Your body is ready to explode into a sexual experience, but you are only watching a film. You are just sitting on a chair and your body is ready for the sex act. The film will go on accelerating, it will go on pushing you. You are aroused, but you cannot do anything. The body is ready to do something but the situation is not appropriate, so a gap is created. You begin to feel as if there is a barrier between you and your body. Because of that barrier, and because of this constant arousal and suppression simultaneously, this acceleration and braking simultaneously, this constant contradiction in your existence, you are diseased.

If you could fall back and be an animal. which is impossible, then you would be whole and healthy. This is a strange fact: animals are not ill in their natural state, but put them in a zoo and they begin to imitate human diseases. No animal goes insane naturally, but in a zoo animals go mad. It has never been reported in the whole history of human understanding that any animal has committed suicide, but in a zoo animals can commit suicide. This is strange, but not strange really, because the moment man begins to force animals into a life that is not natural, then they become divided inside. A division is created, a gap is created, the wholeness is lost.

Man is divided. So what to do? How not to create this gap and how to bring awareness to every cell of the body, to every nook and corner of your being? How to bring awareness? That is the only problem for all systems designed to help you toward enlightenment: how to bring consciousness to your total being so that nothing is unconscious. Many methods have been tried, many methods are possible, so I will talk about some methods for how every cell of your body can become aware. And unless you as a total being become aware, you cannot be in bliss, you cannot be in peace. You will continue to be a madhouse.

Each cell of your body affects you. It has its own working, it has its own learning, its own conditioning. The moment you start, the cell takes over and begins to behave in its own way. Then you are disturbed. "What is happening!" you wonder, "I never intended this; I never thought about it." And you are right. Your desires may have been completely different. But once you give your cells, your body, something to do, it is going to do it in its own way, in its own learned way. Because of this, some scientists think that we cannot change man unless we change the cells.

The behaviorist school of psychology, for example, thinks that Buddha is a failure, that Jesus is a failure, that they are bound to be failures, because without changing the very structure of the body, the chemical structure of the body, nothing can be changed.

These behaviorists – Watson, Pavlov, Skinner – say that if a Buddha is silent, it only means that somehow he has a different chemical constitution and nothing else. If he is silent, if peace surrounds him, if he is never disturbed, never angry, it only shows that somehow the chemicals are lacking that create disturbance, that create anger. So a man like Skinner says that sooner or later we will be able to create a buddha chemically. There is no need for any meditation, there is no need for becoming more aware. The only need is to change chemicals. In a way he is right, but very dangerously right, because if certain chemicals are taken out of your body, your behavior will change. If certain hormones are introduced into your body, your behavior will change. You are a man and you behave like a man, but it is not *you* who behaves like a man; it is only the hormones in you that make you behave like a man. If those hormones are changed and other hormones are introduced that belong to the feminine structure, you will behave like a woman. So it is not really your behavior, it is hormonal behavior. It is not you who is angry but a certain hormone in you. It is not that you are silent and meditative; it is certain hormones or chemicals in you.

So a scientist who thinks like Skinner will say that this is why Buddha is a failure – because he goes on talking about things which are irrelevant. You say to a person, "Don't be angry", but he is filled with chemicals, hormones, which create anger. So for a behaviorist, it is just as if a person has a high fever, a 106-degree fever, and you go on talking about beautiful things to him and say, "Be silent, meditate, don't be feverish!" It looks absurd – what can the man do? Unless you change something in his body the fever will remain. Fever is created by a certain virus, certain chemical phenomena. Unless that is changed, unless the chemistry is changed, he will remain feverish. So there is no need to talk, it is absolutely absurd.

The same is true about anger for a Skinner, for a Pavlov; the same is true about sex. You go on talking about celibacy and the body is filled with sex energy, hormones – that sex energy is not dependent on you. Rather, you are dependent on that energy. So you go on talking about celibacy but nothing is possible through these talks.

They are right in a way, but still, only in a way. They are right that if the chemicals are changed, if every sex hormone is thrown out of your body, you will not be able to be sexual. But you will not become a buddha. You will simply be impotent, incapable. You will lack something.

Buddha is not lacking anything. On the contrary, something new has come to his life. It is not that he has no sex hormones; they are there. So what has happened to him? His consciousness has deepened, and his consciousness has entered even into the sex cells. Now the sex cells are there, but they cannot behave independently. Unless the centre orders them to act, they cannot act. They will remain inactive.

In an impotent person sex cells don't exist. In a buddha they are there and are stronger than in an ordinary person – stronger, because they are not used. Energy is accumulated in them, they are bubbling with energy, but consciousness has penetrated into the cells now. Now the consciousness is not only a starting point; it has become the master.

Skinner's approach may prevail in the coming days, it may become a great force. Just as Marx suddenly became a great force for the outer economy of society, any day Pavlov and Skinner may become a central force for the inner economy of the human body and the human mind. And they can prove whatever they say – they can prove it! But the phenomenon has two aspects.

You see a light bulb – if you destroy the bulb the light will disappear, but it is not that the electricity will disappear. The same happens when you switch off the current: the bulb is intact but the light will again disappear. So the light can disappear in two ways. If you destroy the bulb the electricity will be there, but because there is no medium through which to express it, it cannot become light. If your sex cells are destroyed, sexuality will be in you but with no medium to express itself. This is one way.

Skinner experimented with many animals. Just by operating on a particular gland, a ferocious dog becomes Buddha-like. He sits silently, as if in meditation; you cannot tempt him to be ferocious again. Whatever you do, he will look at you without any anger. It is not that the dog has become a buddha, nor is it that the inner mind has disappeared. It is there all the same, but the medium through which anger can be expressed is absent. This is impotence. The medium has disappeared, not the desire. If the medium is destroyed, when the bulb does not exist, you can say, "Where is your light and where is your electricity?" It is there, but now it is hidden.

The East has been working from the other corner – not trying to destroy the bulb; that is stupid, because if you destroy the bulb then you will not even be aware of the current behind it. Change the current, transform the current, let the current move into a new dimension and the bulb will be there intact alive, but with no light.

Skinner and the behaviorists can prevail because they show such an easy way out. You are angry: you can be operated upon, your chemistry can be changed. You feel sexual; you can be operated upon, your hormones can be changed. Your problems will be solved not by you but by a surgeon, by a pharmacist, by someone else. But whenever a problem is solved by someone else you have missed a very great opportunity, because when *you* solve it you grow. When someone else solves it, you remain the same. The problem can be solved through the body and there will be no problems – but you will also no longer be a human being.

The emphasis of the buddhas is on transformation of consciousness, and the first thing is to create a greater force of awareness inside to help that awareness to spread.

The Upanishads say, "To be established in the sun of awareness is the only lamp."

The sun is very far away. Light takes ten minutes to travel to the earth, and light travels very fast – 186,000 miles per second. It takes ten minutes for the sun to reach the earth; it is very, very far. But in the morning the sun rises, and it reaches even the flowers in your garden. And if your energy becomes a sun deep inside your centre, if your centre becomes a solar centre, if you become aware, centrally aware, if your awareness grows, then the rays of your awareness reach every part of your body, every cell. Then your awareness penetrates every cell of the body.

It is just like when the sun rises in the morning, everything begins to be alive on the earth. Suddenly there is light, and sleep disappears; the monotonous night disappears. Suddenly everything seems to be reborn. The birds begin to sing and they are again on the wing, the flowers open and everything is alive again – just from the touch, just from the warmth, of the sun's rays. So when you have a central consciousness, a central awareness in you, it begins to reach to every pore, to every nook and corner; to every cell it penetrates. And you have many, many cells – trillions of cells in your body. You are a big city, a big nation. Trillions of cells, and now they are all unconscious. Your consciousness has never reached them.

Grow in consciousness and every cell is penetrated. And the moment your consciousness touches the cells, it is different. The very quality changes. A man is asleep – the sun rises and the man is awakened. Is he the same man who was asleep? Is his sleep and awakening the same? There was a closed, dead bud, and the sun has risen, and the bud opens and becomes a flower. Is this flower the same? Something new has penetrated. An aliveness, a capacity to grow and blossom, has appeared. A bird was just asleep, as if dead, like just dead matter – but the sun comes up and the bird is on the wing. Is it the same bird? It is a different phenomenon. Something has touched the bird, and the bird has become alive. Everything was silent and now everything is singing. The morning is a song.

The same phenomenon happens inside the cells of an enlightened person's body. It is known as *buddha-kaya* – the body of an enlightened one, of a buddha. It is a different body.

It is not the same body as you have, not even the same body as Gautam Siddhartha had before he became a buddha.

Buddha is just on the verge of death, and someone asks him, "Are you dying? When you die, where will you be?" Buddha says, "The body that was born will die. But there is another body – the *buddha-kaya*, the body of a buddha, which is neither born, nor can it die. I have left that body which was given to me, that came to me from my parents. Just as a snake leaves the old body every year, I have left it. Now there is the *buddha-kaya* – the buddha-body."

What does this mean? Your body can become a buddha-body. When your consciousness reaches to every cell, the very quality of your being changes, becomes transmuted. Because then every cell is alive, conscious, enlightened. Then there is no slavery. You have become the master. Just by becoming a conscious centre, you become a master.

The Upanishads say, "To be established in the sun of awareness is the only lamp." So why are you taking an earthen lamp to the temple? Take the inner lamp! Why are you burning candles on the altar? They will not help. Kindle the inner candle, become a buddha-body. Let your every cell become conscious; do not allow any part of your being to remain unconscious.

How to create this centre of awareness? I will discuss several methods, but it will be good to start with Buddha. He invented one of the most wonderful methods, a powerful method, for creating an inner fire, an inner sun of awareness. And not only that – the method is such that simultaneously the inner light begins to penetrate to the very cells of the body, to your whole being.

Buddha used breathing as the method – breathing with awareness. The method is known as "Anapanasati Yoga" – the yoga of incoming and outgoing breath awareness. You are breathing, but it is an unconscious thing. And breath is *prana*, breath is the Bergsonian élan *vital*, the vitality, the very vitality, the very light – and it is unconscious. You are not aware of it. If you needed to be aware of it, you might drop dead any moment because then it would be very difficult to breathe.

It would be a problem if you had to "do" breathing. Then you would have to remember constantly in order to do it, and you cannot remember anything even for a single moment! If one moment of breathing is missed, you will be no more. So breathing is unconscious; it does not depend on you. Even if you are in a coma for months together, you will go on breathing.

Buddha used breath as the vehicle to do two things simultaneously: one to create consciousness, and the other to allow that consciousness to penetrate to the very cells of the body. He said, "Breathe consciously." It is not an exercise, a special ritual. It is just making the breath an object of awareness – without any change. There is no need to change your breath; let it be just as it is: natural. Let it be as it is; do not change it. But do something else: when you breathe in, breathe consciously. Let your consciousness move with the ingoing breath. When the breath goes out, move out. Go in, come out. Move consciously with the breath. Let your attention be with the breath; flow with it; do not forget even a single breath.

Buddha is reported to have said that if you can be aware of your breath even for a single hour, you are already enlightened. But not a single breath should be missed. One hour is enough. It looks so small, only a fragment of time, but it is not. When you try it, one hour of awareness will look like millennia because ordinarily you cannot be aware for more than for five or six seconds – and that too only for a very alert person. Otherwise you will miss every second. You will start – the breath is going in. The breath has gone in, and you have gone somewhere else! Suddenly you remember, and you notice that the breath is going out. The breath has gone out and you have moved somewhere else.

To move with the breath means that no thought should be allowed, because thought will take your attention, thought will distract you. So Buddha never says stop thinking, but he says, "Just breathe consciously." Automatically, thinking will stop. You cannot do both, to think and breathe consciously.

A thought comes to your mind, and your attention is withdrawn. A single thought and you become unconscious of your breathing process. So Buddha used a very simple technique and a very vital one. He would say to his disciples, "Do whatsoever you are doing, but do not forget a simple thing: remember the incoming and outgoing breath. Move with it; flow with it." The more you try, the more you make the effort to be aware of the breath, the more you can be conscious. Consciousness will increase by seconds and seconds. It is arduous, a difficult thing – but once you can feel it you are a different person, a different being in a different world.

This works in a double way: when you consciously breathe in and out, by and by you come to your centre, because your breath touches the centre of your being. Every moment that the breath goes in, it touches your centre of being.

Physiologically you think that breath is just for the purification of the blood, that it is just a function of your heart, that it is bodily. You think that it is a function of your circulation, part of a pumping system to refresh your blood circulation, to give to your blood more oxygen that is needed and to throw out carbon dioxide, which is excreta, used stuff, to remove it and replace it.

But this is only the physiological part. If you begin to be aware of your breath, by and by you will go deep – deeper than your heart. And one day you will begin to feel a centre just near your navel. That centre can only be felt if you move with your breath continuously – because the nearer you reach to the centre, the more you tend to lose consciousness.

You can start when the breath is going in. When it is just touching your nose, you can start being alert. The more inward it moves, the more consciousness will become difficult. A thought will come, or some sound or something will happen, and you will move away from your awareness of the breath.

If you can go to the very centre, where for a single moment breath stops and there is a gap, the jump can happen. The breath goes in, the breath goes out – between these two there is a subtle gap. That gap is your centre. When you move with the breath, then only, after a long effort, will you become aware of the gap when there is no movement of the breath, when breath is neither coming nor going. Between two breaths there is a subtle gap, an interval – in that interval you are at the centre.

So breath is used by Buddha as a passage to come nearer and nearer and nearer to the centre. When you move out, be conscious of the breath. Again there is a gap. There are two gaps, one gap inside and one gap outside. The breath goes in, the breath goes out – there is a gap. The breath goes out and the breath goes in – there is a gap. It is even more difficult to be aware of the second gap.

Look at this process. Your centre is in between the incoming breath and the outgoing breath. There is another centre – the cosmic centre. You may call it "god". When the breath goes out and the breath comes in, there is again a gap.

In that gap is the cosmic centre. These two centres are not two different things, but first you will be aware of your inner centre and then you will become aware of your outer centre, and ultimately you will come to know that both these centres are one. Then "out" and "in" lose meaning.

Buddha says move with the breath consciously and you will create a centre of awareness. And once the centre is created, awareness begins to move with your breath into your blood, to the very cells – because every cell needs air and every cell needs oxygen. Every cell, so to speak, breathes – every cell! And now, scientists say, it even seems that the earth breathes. And because of Einstein's concept of an expanding universe, now theoretical scientists say that it seems that the whole universe is breathing.

When you breathe in, your chest expands. When you breathe out, your chest shrinks. Now some scientists say that it seems that the whole universe breathes. When the whole universe is breathing in, it expands. When the whole universe breathes out, it shrinks.

In the old Hindu Puranas, mythological scriptures, it is said that creation is Brahma's incoming breath, and destruction, the end of the world, is the outgoing breath – one breath, one creation.

In a miniature way, in a very atomic way, the same is happening in you. When your awareness becomes so one with breathing, then your breathing takes your awareness to the very cells. Rays now penetrate, and the whole body becomes a buddha-body. Really, then you have no material body at all. You have a body of awareness. This is what is meant by the Upanishadic sutra, "To be established in the sun of awareness . . ." this is the only lamp.

Just like we are learning about Buddha's method, it will be good to understand another method. Tantra has used sex; that is again another vital force. If you want to go deep, you have to use the vital forces, the deepest in you. Tantra uses sex. When you are in a sex act, you are very near to the centre of creation, to the very source of life. If you can go into a sex act consciously, it becomes meditation.

It is very difficult – more difficult than breath. You can breathe consciously in small measure, of course, but the very phenomenon of sex requires your unconsciousness. If you become conscious you will lose your sexual desire and lust. If you become conscious, then there will be no sexual desire inside. So Tantra has done the most difficult thing in the world. In the history of experiments with consciousness, Tantra goes the deepest.

But, of course one can deceive, and with Tantra deception is very easy because no one other than you knows what the fact is. No one else can know. But only one in a hundred can succeed in the Tantric method of awareness, because sex needs unconsciousness. So a Tantric, a disciple of Tantra, has to work with sex, sex desire, just like with breathing. He has to be conscious of it; when actually going into the sex act, he has to be conscious.

Your very body, the sex energy, comes to a peak to explode. The Tantric seeker comes to the peak consciously, and there is a method to judge. If sexual release happens automatically and you are not the master, then you are not conscious of it. Then the unconscious has taken over. Sex comes to a peak, and then you cannot do anything but release. That release is not done by you. You can start a sexual process, but you can never end it. The end is always taken over by the unconscious.

If you can retain the peak and if it becomes your conscious act to release it or not to release it, if you can come back from the peak without release, or if you can maintain that peak for hours together – if it is your conscious act – then you are the master. And if someone can come to a sexual peak, just on the verge of orgasm, and can retain it and be conscious of it, suddenly he becomes aware of the deepest centre inside – suddenly. And it is not only that he is aware of the deepest centre inside of himself; he is also aware of the centre of his partner, the deepest centre.

That is why a Tantra practitioner, if he is a man, will always worship the partner. The partner is not just a sex object, she is divine; she is a goddess. And the act is not carnal at all. If you can go into it consciously, it is the deepest spiritual act possible. But the deepest is bound to be virtually impossible.

So, use either breath or sex. Breath is the easiest. It will be difficult to use the Tantra method. The mind would like to use it, but it will be difficult. Only the breath process is simple. And for the coming age, I think Buddha's method will be very helpful. It is moderate, easy, not very dangerous.

And there are many more methods. With any method you can be established in that inner light. And once you are established, your light begins to flow to your body cells. Then your whole mechanism is refreshed and you have a buddha-body, an enlightened one's body.

A friend, who has a PhD in computing, and whose thesis was on artificial intelligence, says that man is a biochemical computer and nothing more. Buddha has said that all things are composite and there is no self, no soul, no spirit, no "I", which seems to agree with my friend's viewpoint. Could you please help me, because I feel that there is something missing from these views but I can't see it myself.

Man certainly is a bio-computer, but something more too. About most people it can be said that they are only bio-computers and nothing more. Ordinarily one is only the body and the mind, and both are composites. Unless one moves into meditation, one cannot find that which is something more, something transcendental to body and mind.

The psychologists, particularly the behaviorists, have been studying man for half a century, but they study the ordinary man and of course their thesis is proved by all their studies. The ordinary man, the unconscious man, has nothing more in him than the body–mind composite. The body is the outer side of the mind and the mind is the inner side of the body. Both are born and both will die one day.

But there is something more. That something more makes a person awakened, enlightened, a Buddha, a Christ. But a Buddha or a Christ is not available to be studied by Pavlov, Skinner, Delgado and others. Their study is about the unconscious man, and of course when you study the unconscious man you will not find anything transcendental in him. The transcendental exists in the unconscious man only as a potential, as a possibility; it is not yet realized, it is not yet a reality. Hence you cannot study it.

You can study it only in a Buddha – but even then, study is obviously very difficult, close to impossible, because what you will study in a Buddha will again be his behavior. If you are determined that there is nothing more, if you have already concluded, then even in his behavior you will see only mechanical reactions; you will not see his spontaneity. To see that spontaneity you have also to become a participant in meditation.

Psychology can become only a real psychology when meditation becomes its foundation. The word "psychology"

171

means the science of the soul. Modern psychology is not yet a science of the soul.

Buddha certainly has denied the self, the ego, the "I". He has not denied the soul, and the self and the soul are not synonymous. He denies the self because the self exists only in the unconscious man. The unconscious man needs a certain idea of "I"; otherwise he will be without a centre. He does not know his real centre. He has to invent a false centre so that he can at least function in the world; otherwise his functioning will become impossible. He needs a certain idea of "I".

You must have heard about Descartes' famous statement: "*Cogito ergo sum* – I think, therefore I am."

A professor, teaching the philosophy of Descartes, was asked by a student, "Sir, I think, but how do I know that I am?"

The professor pretended to peer around the classroom. "Who is asking the question?" he said.

"I am," replied the student.

One needs a certain idea of "I"; otherwise functioning will become impossible. So because we don't know the real "I" we substitute it with a false "I" – something invented, a composite.

Buddha denies the self because to him "self" simply is another name for the ego with a little colour of spirituality; otherwise there is no difference. His word is *anatta*. *Atta* means "self", *anatta* means "no-self". But he is not denying the soul. In fact when the self is completely dropped, then only you will come to know the soul. But Buddha does not say anything about it because nothing can be said.

His approach is *via negativa*. He says: you are not the body, you are not the mind, you are not the self. He goes on denying, eliminating; he eliminates everything that you can conceive of, and then he does not say anything about what is left. That which is left is your reality – that utterly pure sky without clouds, no thought, no identity, no emotion, no desire, no ego, nothing is left. All clouds have disappeared . . . just the pure sky.

It is inexpressible, unnameable, indefinable. That's why he keeps absolutely silent about it. He knows that if anything is said about it you will immediately jump back to your old idea of the self. If he says, "There is a soul in you", what are you going to understand? You will think, "He calls it soul and we call it self – it is the same. The supreme self maybe, the spiritual self; it is not just ordinary ego." But spiritual or unspiritual, the idea of being a separate entity is the point. Buddha denies that you are a separate entity from the whole. You are one with the organic unity of existence, so there is no need to say anything about your separateness. Even the word "soul" will give you a certain idea of separateness; you are bound to understand it in your own unconscious way.

Your friend says that man is a biochemical computer and nothing more – can a biochemical computer say that? Can a biochemical computer deny the self, the soul? No bio-computer or any other kind of computer has any idea of self or no-self. Your friend is doing it – certainly he is not a biochemical computer. No biochemical computer can write a thesis on artificial intelligence! Do you think artificial intelligence can write a thesis about artificial intelligence? Something more is needed.

It is wrong to think that Buddha agrees with his viewpoint – not at all. Buddha's experience is of meditation. Without meditation nobody can have any idea what Buddha is talking about. Your friend's observation is from the standpoint of a scientific onlooker; it is not his experience, it is his observation. He is studying biochemical computers, artificial intelligence, from the outside. Who is studying?

Can you conceive of two computers studying each other? The computer can know only that which has been fed into it; it cannot have more than that. The information has to be given to it, then it keeps it in its memory – it is a memory system. It can do miracles as far as mathematics is concerned. A computer can be far more efficient than any Albert Einstein as far as mathematics is concerned, but a computer cannot be a meditator. Can you imagine a computer just sitting silently doing nothing, the spring comes and the grass grows by itself . . .?

There are many qualities that are impossible for the computer. A computer cannot be in love. You can keep many computers together – they will not fall in love! A computer cannot have any experience of beauty, a computer cannot know any bliss. A computer cannot have any awareness. A computer is incapable of feeling silence. These are the qualities that prove that man has something more than artificial intelligence.

Artificial intelligence can do scientific work, mathematical work, calculation – and very quickly and efficiently, because it is a machine. But a machine cannot be aware of what it is doing. A computer cannot feel boredom, a computer cannot feel meaninglessness, a computer cannot experience anguish. A computer cannot start an enquiry about truth, it cannot renounce the world and become a *sannyasin*, it cannot go to the mountains or to the monasteries. It cannot conceive of anything beyond the mechanical – and all that is significant is beyond the mechanical.

Part III

THE PSYCHOLOGY OF THE BUDDHAS IN ACTION

The psychology of the buddhas is the yoga, the discipline, the inner journey, the science – or whatsoever you want to call it – of knowing that there is something inside you that can only be known through going there, through *being* there. No other way, no other approach is possible.

Awareness is the Key

The unconscious can be transformed only through awareness. It is difficult, but there is no other way. There are many methods for being aware, but awareness is necessary. You can use methods to be aware, but you will have to be aware.

If someone asks whether there is any method to dispel darkness except by light, however difficult it may be that is the only way – because darkness is simply the absence of light. So you have to create the presence of light, and then darkness is not there.

Unconsciousness is nothing but an absence – the absence of consciousness. It is not something positive in itself, so you cannot do anything except be aware. If unconsciousness were something in its own right, then it would be a different matter – but it is not. Unconsciousness doesn't mean something; it only means not consciousness. It is just an absence. It has no existence in itself; in itself it is not. The word "unconscious" simply shows the absence of consciousness and nothing else. When we say "darkness" the word is misleading, because the moment we say "darkness" it appears that darkness is something that is there. It is not, so you cannot do anything with darkness directly – or can you?

You may not have observed the fact, but with darkness you cannot do anything directly. Whatever you want to do with darkness you will have to do with light, not with darkness. If you want darkness, then turn off the light. If you don't want darkness, then turn on the light. But you cannot do anything directly with darkness; you will have to go via light.

Why can you not go directly? You cannot go directly because there is nothing like darkness, so you cannot touch it directly. You have to do something with light, and then you have done something with darkness.

If light is there, then darkness is not there. If light is not there, then darkness is there. You can bring light into this room, but you cannot bring darkness. You can take light out from this room, but you cannot take darkness out from this room. There exists no connection between you and darkness. Why? If darkness were there then man could be related somehow, but darkness is not there.

Language gives you a fallacious idea that darkness is something. Darkness is a negative term. It exists not. It connotes only that light is not there – nothing more – and the same is with unconsciousness. So when you ask what to do other than to be aware, you ask an irrelevant question. You will have to be aware; you cannot do anything else.

Of course, there are many methods for being aware – that is a different thing. There are many ways to create light, but light will have to be created. You can create a fire and there will be no darkness. You can use a kerosene lamp and there will be no darkness. You can use electricity and there will be no darkness. But whatever the case, whatever the method of producing light, light has to be produced.

Light is a must – and all meditation techniques are just methods to produce awareness. They are not alternatives, remember; they are not alternatives to awareness – there are none. Awareness is the only possibility for dispelling darkness, for dispelling unconsciousness. But how to create awareness? The purest method is to be aware inside of what happens on the boundary line between the unconscious and the conscious – to be aware there.

Anger is there – anger is produced in darkness. Anger has its roots in the unconscious; it is only the branches and leaves that come into the conscious. The roots, the seeds, the energy sources of anger are in the unconscious. You become aware only of the faraway branches. Be conscious of these branches – the more conscious you are, the more you will be capable of looking into the darkness.

Have you noticed that if you look deeply into the darkness for a certain time, a certain dim light begins to appear? If you concentrate in the darkness, you begin to feel and you begin to see. You can train yourself, and then in darkness itself there is a certain amount of light – because, really, in this world nothing can be absolute. Everything is relative. When we say "darkness" it doesn't mean absolute darkness. It only means that there is less light. If you practice to be able to see in the darkness, you will be capable of seeing. Look, focus yourself in the darkness and then, by and by, your eyes will be strengthened and you will begin to see.

Inner darkness, unconsciousness, is the same. Look into it – but you can look only if you are not active. If you begin to act, your mind is distracted. Don't act inside. Anger is there – don't act. Don't condemn, don't appreciate, don't indulge in it and don't suppress it. Don't do anything – just look at it, observe it.

Understand the distinction. What happens ordinarily is just the reverse. If you are angry, then your mind becomes focused on the cause of anger outside – always! Someone has insulted you and you are angry. Now, there are three things going on: the cause of anger outside, the source of anger inside, and you are in between these two. Anger is your energy inside. The cause that has provoked your energy to come up is outside. And you are in between. The natural way of the mind is not to be aware of the source, but to be focused on the cause outside. Whenever you are angry, you are in deep concentration on the cause outside.

The Jain master Mahavir has called anger a sort of meditation. He has named it *roudra dhyan* – meditation on negative attitudes. It is, because you are so concentrated; really, when you are in deep anger you are so concentrated that the whole world disappears and only the cause of anger is in focus. Your total energy is focused on the cause of anger, and you are so focused on the cause that you forget yourself completely. That's why in anger you can do things and later on, you say, "I did them in spite of myself." *You* were not there.

For awareness you have to take an about-turn. You have to concentrate not on the cause outside, but on the source inside. Forget the cause. Close your eyes, and go deep and dig into the source. Then you can use the same energy that would have been wasted on someone outside – the energy moves inwards.

Anger has much energy. Anger *is* energy, the purest of fires inside. Don't waste it outside.

Take another example. You are feeling sexual: sex is again energy, fire. But whenever you feel sexual, again you are focused on someone outside, not on the source. You begin to think of someone – of the lover, of the beloved, A-B-C-D – but when you are filled with sex your focus is always on the other. You are dissipating energy. Not only in the sexual act do you dissipate energy, but in sexual thinking you dissipate it even more because a sexual act is a momentary thing. It comes to a peak, the energy is released, and you are thrown back. But sexual thinking can be there all the time. You can continue releasing your energy in sexual thinking, you can dissipate it.

And everyone is dissipating energy. Ninety per cent of our thinking is sexual. Whatever you are doing outside, sex is a constant concern inside – you may not even be aware of it.

You are sitting in a room and a woman enters: your posture changes suddenly. Your spine is more erect, your breathing changes, your blood pressure is different. You may not be aware at all of what has happened, but your whole body has reacted sexually. You were one person when the woman was not there; now you are a different person.

An all-male group is a different group, and an all-female group is a different group. Let one male come into the room, or one female, and the whole energy pattern of the group changes suddenly. You may not be conscious of it, but when your mind is focused on someone, your energy begins to flow.

When you feel sexual, look at the source, not at the cause – remember this. Science is more concerned with the cause, and awareness is more concerned with the source. The source is always inside; the cause is always outside. With the cause you are getting involved in a chain reaction. With the cause you are connected with your environment. With the source you are connected with yourself. So remember this – this is the purest method to change unconscious energy into conscious energy. Take an about-turn – look inside! It is going to be difficult because our way of looking has become fixed in a certain pattern. We are like a person whose neck is paralysed, who cannot turn and look back. Our eyes have become fixed; we have been looking outside for lives together, for millennia, so we don't know how to look inside.

Do this: whenever something happens in your mind, follow it to the source. Anger is there – a sudden flash has come to you: close your eyes and meditate on it. From where is this anger arising? Never ask the question, who has made this happen, who has made you angry – that is a wrong question. Ask which energy in you is transforming into anger – from where is this anger coming up, bubbling up? What is the source inside from where this energy is coming?

Are you aware that in anger you can do something that you cannot do when you are not in anger? A person in anger can throw a big stone easily. When he is not angry he cannot even lift it. He has so much energy when he is angry; a hidden source is now with him. So if a man is mad, he becomes very strong. Why? From where is this energy coming? It is not coming from anything outside. Now all his sources are burning simultaneously – anger, sex, everything is burning simultaneously. Every source of energy is available.

Be concerned with seeing from where the anger is bubbling up, from where the sexual desire has come in. Follow it, take steps backwards. Meditate silently and go with the anger to the roots. It is difficult but it is not impossible. It is not easy – it is not going to be easy because it is a fight against a long-rooted habit. The whole past has to be broken and you have to do something new, which you have never done before. It is just the weight of sheer habit which will create the difficulty. But try it, and then you are creating a new direction for energy to move. You are becoming a circle, and in a circle energy is never dissipated.

If my energy comes up and moves outside, it can never become a circle; it is simply dissipated. If an inward movement is there, then the same energy that was going out turns back in upon itself. My meditation leads this energy back to the same source from where the anger was coming and it becomes a circle. This inner circle is the strength of a buddha. The sex energy, not moving to someone else, moves back to its own source. This circle of sex energy is the strength of a buddha.

We are weaklings not because we have less energy than a buddha: we have the same amount of energy, everyone is born with the same energy quanta, but we are accustomed to dissipating it. It simply moves away from us and never comes back. It cannot come back! Once it is out of you, it can never come back – it is gone.

A word arises in me and I speak it out; it has flown away. It is not going to come back to me, and the energy that was used in producing it, that was used in throwing it away, is dissipated. A word arises in me and I don't throw it out; I remain silent. Then the word moves and moves and moves, and falls into the original source again. The energy has been re-consumed.

Silence is energy. Not to be angry is energy. But this is not suppression. If you suppress anger, you have used up your energy again. Don't suppress – observe and follow. Don't fight – just move backwards with the anger. This is the purest method of awareness.

And certain other things can be used. For beginners, certain devices are possible. So I will talk about three devices. One type of device is based on body awareness. Forget anger, forget sex – they are difficult to deal with, and when you are in them you become so mad that you cannot meditate. When you are angry you cannot meditate; you cannot even think about meditation. You are just mad. So forget it; it is difficult. Then use your own body as a device for awareness.

Buddha has said that when you walk, walk consciously. When you breathe, breathe consciously. The Buddhist method is known as Anapanasati Yoga – the yoga of the incoming and outgoing breath, incoming and outgoing breath awareness. The breath comes in: move with the breath; know, be aware, that the breath is moving in. When the breath has gone out again, move with it. Be in, be out, with the breath.

Anger is difficult, sex is difficult – breath is not so difficult. Move with the breath. Don't allow any breath to be in or out without consciousness. This is a meditation. Now you will be focused on breathing, and when you are focused on breathing, thoughts stop automatically. You cannot think, because the moment you think, your consciousness moves from breath to thought. You have missed breathing.

Try this and you will know. When you are aware of breathing, thoughts cease. The same energy which is used for thoughts is being used in being aware of breath. If you start thinking, you will lose track of the breath, you will forget, and you will think. You cannot do both simultaneously.

If you are following breathing, it is a long process. One has to go into it deeply. It takes a minimum of three months and a maximum of three years. If it is done continuously 24 hours a day . . . it is a method for monks, those who have given up everything; only they can watch their breathing 24 hours a day. That's why Buddhist monks and other traditions of monks reduce their living to the minimum so that no disturbance is there. They will beg for their food and they will sleep under a tree – that's all. Their whole time is devoted to some inner practice of being aware – for example, of breath.

A Buddhist monk has to be continuously aware of his breath. The silence that you see on a Buddhist monk's face is the silence of the awareness of breathing and nothing else. If you become aware your face will become silent, because if thoughts are not there your face cannot show anxiety, thinking. Your face becomes relaxed. Continuous awareness of breathing will stop the mind. The continuously troubled mind will stop. And if the mind stops and you are simply aware of breathing, if the mind is not functioning, you cannot be angry, you cannot be sexual.

Sex or anger or greed or jealousy or envy – anything like that needs the mechanism of the mind for support. If the mechanism stops, you cannot do anything. This again leads to the same thing as the first method – now the energy that was used in sex, in anger, in greed, in ambition, has no outlet. You go on continuously being concerned with breathing, day and night. Buddha has said, "Even in sleep try to be aware of breathing." It will be difficult in the beginning, but if you can be aware in the day, then by and by this will penetrate into your sleep.

Anything penetrates into sleep if it has gone deep in the mind in the day. If you have been worried about a certain thing in the day, it gets into the sleep. If you were thinking continuously about sex, it gets into the sleep. If you were angry the whole day, anger gets into the sleep. So Buddha says there is no difficulty about it – if a person is continuously concerned with breathing and awareness of the breathing, ultimately it penetrates into the sleep. You cannot dream then. If your awareness is there, of incoming breath and outgoing breath, then in sleep you cannot dream.

The moment you dream, this awareness will not be there. If awareness is there, dreams are impossible. So a Buddhist monk asleep is not just like you. His sleep has a different quality. It has a different depth and a certain awareness in it.

Ananda said to Buddha, "I have observed you for years and years together. It seems like a miracle: you sleep as if you are awake. You are in the same posture the whole night." The hand would not move from the place where it had been put; the leg would remain in the same posture. Buddha would sleep in the same posture the whole night. Not a single movement! For nights together Ananda would sit and watch and wonder, "What type of sleep is this!" Buddha would not move. He would be as if a dead body, and he would wake up in the same posture in which he went to sleep. Ananda asked, "What are you doing? Were you asleep or not? You never move!"

Buddha said, "A day will come, Ananda, when you will know. This shows that you are not practicing Anapanasati Yoga rightly; it shows only this. Otherwise this question would not have arisen. You are not practicing Anapanasati Yoga – if you are continuously aware of your breath in the day, it is impossible not to be conscious of it in the night. And if the mind is concerned with awareness, dreams cannot penetrate. And if there are no dreams, mind is clear, transparent. Your body is asleep, but you are not. Your body is relaxing, you are aware – the flame is there inside. So, Ananda," Buddha is reported to have said, "I am not asleep – only the body is sleep. I am aware! and not only in sleep. Ananda – when I die, you will see: I will be aware, only the body will die."

Practice awareness with breathing; then you will be capable of penetrating. Or practice awareness with body movements. Buddha has a word for it: he calls it "mindfulness". He says, "Walk mindfully." We walk without any mind in it.

A certain man was sitting before Buddha when he was talking one day. He was moving his leg and a toe unnecessarily. There was no reason for it. Buddha stopped talking and asked that man, "Why are you moving your leg? Why are you moving your toe?" Suddenly, as the Buddha asked, the man stopped. Then Buddha asked, "Why have you stopped so suddenly?"

The man said, "Why, I was not even aware that I was moving my toe or my leg! I was not aware! The moment you asked, I became aware."

Buddha said, "What nonsense! Your leg is moving and you are not aware? So what are you doing with your body? Are you an alive man or dead? This is your leg, this is your toe, and it goes on moving and you are not even aware? Then of what are you aware? You can kill a man and you can say, 'I was not aware.'" And, really, those who kill are not aware. It is difficult to kill someone when you are aware.

Buddha would say, "Move, walk, but be filled with consciousness. Know inwardly you are walking." You are not to use any words; you are not to use any thoughts. You are not to say inside, "I am walking", because if you say it then you are not aware of walking – you have become aware of your thought, and you have missed walking. Just be somatically aware – not mentally. Just feel that you are walking. Create a somatic awareness, a sensitivity, so that you can feel directly without mind coming in.

The wind is blowing – you are feeling it. Don't use words. Just feel, and be mindful of the feeling. You are lying down on the beach, and the sand is cool, deeply cool. Feel it! – don't use words. Just feel it – the coolness of it, the penetrating coolness of it. Just feel! Be conscious of it; don't use words. Don't say, "The sand is very cool." The moment you say it you have missed an existential moment. You have become intellectual about it.

You are with your lover or with your beloved: feel the presence; don't use words. Just feel the warmth, the love flowing. Just feel the oneness that has happened. Don't use words. Don't say, "I love you"; you will have destroyed it. The mind has come in. And the moment you say, "I love you", it has become a past memory. Just feel without words. Anything felt without words, felt totally without the mind coming in, will give you a mindfulness.

You are eating: eat mindfully; taste everything mindfully. Don't use words. The taste is itself such a great and penetrating thing. Don't use words and don't destroy it. Feel it to the core. You are drinking water: feel it passing through the throat; don't use words. Just feel it; be mindful about it. The movement of the water, the coolness, the disappearing thirst, the satisfaction that follows – feel it!

You are sitting in the sun: feel the warmth; don't use words. The sun is touching you. There is a deep communion. Feel it! In this way, somatic awareness, bodily awareness, is developed. If you develop a bodily awareness, again mind comes to a stop. Mind is not needed. And if mind stops, you are again thrown into the deep unconscious. With a very, very deep alertness you can penetrate. Now you have a light with you, and the darkness disappears.

Those who are bodily oriented, for them it is good to be somatically mindful. For those who are not bodily oriented it is better to be conscious of breathing.

There are many, many methods. But any method is just an effort toward awareness. You cannot escape awareness. You can start from wherever you like, but awareness is the key.

Modern Methods for Modern Man

Why did you create new, active meditation techniques like your Kundalini Meditation and Dynamic Meditation, even though there is a tradition already including hundreds of techniques from yoga, Sufism, Buddhism, etc.?

The ancient methods of meditation were all developed in the East. They never considered the Western man; the Western man was excluded. I am creating techniques which are not only for the Eastern man, but which are simply for every man – Eastern or Western.

There is a difference between the Eastern tradition and the Western tradition – and it is the tradition that creates the mind. For example, the Eastern mind is very patient – thousands of years of teaching to remain patient, whatever the conditions may be.

The Western mind is very impatient. The same methods of technique cannot be applicable to both.

The Eastern mind has been conditioned to keep a certain equilibrium in success or in failure, in richness or in poverty, in sickness or in health, in life or in death. The Western mind has no idea of such equilibrium; it gets too disturbed. With success it gets disturbed; it starts feeling at the top of the world, starts feeling a certain superiority complex. In failure it goes to the other extreme; it falls into the seventh hell. It is miserable, in deep anguish, and it feels a tremendous inferiority complex. It is torn apart.

And life consists of both. There are moments which are beautiful, and there are moments which are ugly. There are moments when you are in love, there are moments when you are in anger, in hatred. The Western mind simply goes with the situation. It is always in a turmoil. The Eastern mind has learned . . . it is a conditioning, it is not a revolution, it is only a training, a discipline, it is a practice. Underneath, it is the same, but a thick conditioning makes it keep a certain balance.

The Eastern mind is very slow because there is no point in being speedy; life takes its own course and everything is determined by fate, so what you get, you don't get by your speed, your hurry. What you get, you get because it is already destined. So there is no question of being in a hurry. Whenever something is going to happen, it is going to happen – neither one second before nor one second after it.

This has created a very slow flow in the East. It seems almost as if the river is not flowing; it is so slow that you cannot detect the flow. Moreover, the Eastern conditioning is that you have already lived millions of lives, and there are millions ahead to be lived, so the life span is not only 70 years; the life span is vast and enormous. There is no hurry; there is so much time available: why should you be in a hurry? If it does not happen in this life, it may happen in some other life.

The Western mind is very speedy, fast, because the conditioning is for only one life – 70 years – and so much to do. One third of your life goes into sleep, one third of your life goes into education, training – what is left?

Much of it goes into earning your livelihood. If you count everything, you will be surprised: out of 70 years you cannot even have seven years left for something that you want to do. Naturally there is hurry, a mad rush, so mad that one forgets where one is going. All that you remember is whether you are going with speed or not. The means becomes the end.

In the same way, in different directions . . . the Eastern mind has cultivated itself differently than the Western mind. Those 112 methods of meditation developed in the East have never taken account of the Western man; they were not developed for the Western man. The Western man was not yet available. The time that *Vigyan Bhairav Tantra* was written – in which those 112 techniques have come to perfection – is five to ten thousand years before us.

At that time there was no Western man, no Western society, no Western culture. The West was still barbarous, primitive, not worth taking into account. The East was the whole world, at the pinnacle of its growth, richness, civilization.

My methods of meditation have been developed out of an absolute necessity. I want the distinction between the West and the East to be dissolved.

After Shiva's *Vigyan Bhairav Tantra*, in these five or ten thousand years, nobody has developed a single new method. But I have been watching the differences between East and West: the same method cannot be applied immediately to both. First, the Eastern and the Western mind have to be brought into a similar state. Those techniques of Dynamic Meditation, Kundalini Meditation, and others, are all cathartic; their basis is catharsis.

You have to throw out all the junk that your mind is full of. Unless you are unloaded you cannot sit silently. It is just as if you tell a child to sit silently in the corner of the room. It is very difficult, he is so full of energy. You are repressing a volcano! The best way is, first tell him, "Go run outside around the house ten times; then come and sit down in the corner."

Then it is possible, you have made it possible. He himself wants to sit down now, to relax. He is tired, he is exhausted; now, sitting there, he is not repressing his energy, he has expressed his energy by running around the house ten times. Now he is more at ease.

The cathartic methods are simply to throw out all your impatience, your speediness, your hurry, your repressions.

One more factor has to be remembered: that these are absolutely necessary for the Western man before he can do something like *vipassana* – just sitting silently doing nothing and the grass grows by itself. But you have to be sitting silently, doing nothing – that is a basic condition for the grass to grow by itself. If you cannot sit silently doing nothing, you are going to disturb the grass.

I have always loved gardens, and wherever I have lived I have created beautiful gardens, lawns. I used to talk to people sitting on my lawn, and I became aware that they were all pulling the grass out . . . just hectic energy. If they had nothing to do they would simply pull the grass. I had to tell them, "If you go on doing this, then you will have to sit inside the room. I cannot allow you to destroy my lawn."

They would stop themselves for a while, and as they started listening to me, again unconsciously, their hands would start pulling at the grass. So sitting silently doing nothing is not really just sitting silently and doing nothing. It is doing a big favour to the grass. Unless you are not doing anything, the grass cannot grow; you will stop it, you will pull it out, you will disturb it.

So these methods are absolutely necessary for the Western mind. But a new factor has also entered: they have become necessary for the Eastern mind too. The mind for which Shiva wrote those 112 methods of meditation no longer exists – even in the East now. The Western influence has been tremendous. Things have changed.

In Shiva's time there was no Western civilization. The East was at its peak of glory; it was called "a golden bird". It had all the luxuries and comforts: it was really affluent.

Now the situation is reversed: the East has been in slavery for two thousand years, exploited by almost everyone in the world, invaded by a dozen countries, continuously looted, raped, burnt. It is now a beggar.

And three hundred years of British rule in India have destroyed India's own educational system – which was a totally different thing. The British forced the Eastern mind to be educated according to Western standards. They have almost turned the Eastern intelligentsia into a second-grade Western intelligentsia. They have given their disease of speediness, of hurry, of impatience, of continuous anguish, anxiety, to the East.

If you see the temples of Khajuraho or the temples of Konarak, you can see the East in its true colours. Just in Khajuraho there were one hundred temples; only 30 have survived, 70 have been destroyed by Mohammedans. Thousands of temples of tremendous beauty and sculpture have been destroyed. These 30 survived; it was just coincidence, because they were part of a forest. Perhaps the invaders forgot about them.

But the British influence on the Indian mind was so great that even a man like Mahatma Gandhi wanted these 30 temples to be covered with mud so that nobody could see them. Just to think of the people who had created those hundred temples . . . each temple must have taken centuries to build. They are so delicate in structure, so proportionate and so beautiful, that there exists nothing parallel to them on the earth.

And you can imagine that temples don't exist alone; if there were a hundred temples, there must have been a city of thousands of people; otherwise a hundred temples are meaningless. Where are those people? With the temples those people have been massacred.

And those temples I take as an example, because their sculpture will look pornographic to the Western mind; to Mahatma Gandhi it also looked pornographic.

India owes so much to Rabindranath Tagore. He was the man who prevented Mahatma Gandhi and other politicians who were ready to cover the temples, to hide them from people's eyes. Rabindranath Tagore said, "This is absolutely stupid. They are not pornographic, they are utterly beautiful."

There is a very delicate line between pornography and beauty. A naked woman is not necessarily pornographic; a naked man is not necessarily pornographic. A beautiful man, a beautiful woman, naked, can be examples of beauty, of health, of proportion. They are the most glorious products of nature. If a deer can be naked and beautiful – and nobody thinks the deer is pornographic – then why should it be that a naked man or woman cannot be just seen as beautiful?

There were ladies in the time of Queen Victoria in England who covered the legs of the chairs with cloth because legs should not be left naked – chairs' legs! But because they are called legs, it was thought uncivilized, uncultured, to leave them naked. There was a movement in Victoria's time urging that people who take their dogs for a walk should cover them with cloth. The dogs should not be naked . . . as if nakedness itself is pornographic. It is the pornographic mind.

I have been to Khajuraho hundreds of times, and I have not seen a single sculpture as pornographic. A naked picture or a naked statue becomes pornography if it provokes your sexuality. That's the only criterion: if it provokes your sexuality, if it is an incentive to your sexual instinct. But that is not the case with Khajuraho. In fact the temples were made for just the opposite purpose. They were made to meditate on man and woman making love. And the stones have come alive. The people who have made them must have been the greatest artists the world has known.

They were made to meditate upon, they were objects for meditation. The place was a temple, and meditators were sitting around just looking at the sculptures and watching within themselves to see whether there was any sexual desire arising. This was the criterion: when they found there was no sexual desire arising, it was a certificate for them to enter the temples. All these sculptures are outside the temple, on the walls outside; inside there are no nude statues.

But this was a necessary step, first for people to meditate. And when they were clear that there was no desire – on the contrary, those statues had made their ordinary desire for sex subside – then they were capable of entering into the temple; otherwise they should not enter the temple. That would be a profanity – having such a desire inside and entering the temple. It would be making the temple dirty – you would be insulting the temple.

The people who created these temples created a tremendous, voluminous literature also. The East never used to be repressive of sexuality. Before Buddha and Mahavira, the East was never repressive of sexuality. It was with Buddha and Mahavira that for the first time celibacy became spiritual. Otherwise, before Buddha and Mahavira, all the seers of the Upanishads, of the Vedas, were married people; they were not celibate, they had children.

And they were not people who had renounced the world; they had all the luxuries and all the comforts. They lived in the forests, but they had everything presented to them by their students, by the kings, by their lovers. And their ashrams, their schools, their academies in the forest were very affluent.

With Buddha and Mahavira the East began a sick tradition of celibacy, of repression. And when Christianity came into India, there came a very strong trend of repressiveness. These three hundred years of Christianity have made the Eastern mind almost as repressive as the Western mind.

So now my methods are applicable to both. I call them preliminary methods. They are to destroy everything that can prevent you from going into a silent meditation. Once Dynamic Meditation or Kundalini Meditation succeeds, you are clean. You have erased repressiveness. You have erased the speediness, the hurry, the impatience. Now it is possible for you to enter the temple.

It is for this reason that I spoke about the acceptance of sex, because without the acceptance of sex, you cannot get rid of repression. And I want you to be completely clean, natural. I want you to be in a state where those 112 methods can be applicable to you.

This is my reason for devising these methods – these are simply cleansing methods.

I have also included the Western therapeutic methods because the Western mind, and under its influence, the Eastern mind, both have become sick. It is a rare phenomenon today to find a healthy mind. Everybody is feeling a certain kind of nausea, a mental nausea, a certain emptiness, which is like a wound hurting. Everybody is having his life turned into a nightmare. Everybody is worried, too much afraid of death; not only afraid of death but also afraid of life.

People are living half-heartedly, people are living in a lukewarm way: not intensely like Zorba the Greek, not with a healthy flavour but with a sick mind. One has to live, so they are living. One has to love, so they are loving. One has to do this, to be like this, so they are following; otherwise there is no incentive coming from their own being.

They are not overflowing with energy. They are not risking anything to live totally. They are not adventurous – and without being adventurous, one is not healthy. Adventure is the criterion, enquiry into the unknown is the criterion. People are not young, from childhood they simply become old. Youth never happens.

The Western therapeutic methods cannot help you to grow spiritually, but they can prepare the ground. They cannot sow the seeds of flowers but they can prepare the ground – which is a necessity. This was one reason why I included therapies in my work.

There is also another reason: I want a meeting of East and West.

The East has developed meditative methods; the West has not developed meditative methods, the West has developed psychotherapies. If we want the Western mind to be interested in meditation methods, if you want the Eastern mind to come closer to the Western, then there has to be something of give and take. It should not be just Eastern – something from the Western evolution should be included. And I find those therapies are immensely helpful. They can't go far, but as far as they go, it is good. Where they stop, meditations can take over.

But the Western mind should feel that something of its own development has been included in the meeting, in the merger; it should not be one-sided. And these therapies are significant; they cannot harm, they can only help. I have used them for years with tremendous success. They have helped people to cleanse their beings, prepared them to be ready to enter into the temple of meditation. My effort is to dissolve the separation between East and West. The earth should be one, not only politically but spiritually too.

Some people think that this is a clever way of brainwashing. It is something more: it is mindwashing, not brainwashing. Brainwashing is very superficial. The brain is the mechanism that the mind uses. You can wash the brain very easily – just any mechanism can be washed and cleaned and lubricated. But if the mind which is behind the brain is polluted, is dirty, is full of repressed desires, is full of ugliness, soon the brain will be full of all those ugly things.

And I don't see that there is anything wrong in it – washing is always good! I believe in dry-cleaning. I don't use old methods of washing. And yes, people will feel cheated that their mind has been taken away, and that was the only precious thing they had. This will be only in the beginning. Once the mind is taken away, they will be surprised that behind the mind is their real treasure. And the mind was only a mirror, it was reflecting the treasure, but it had no treasure in itself. The treasure is behind the mind – that is your being.

Is there any particular method of meditation useful for treatment of a particular type of mental illness?

Modern psychiatry is rooted and based in illness – it knows nothing about wellness. Modern psychology and all its branches are basically following the medical model. That's where Sigmund Freud missed. He contributed something immensely valuable, but still he missed the whole point. He was too interested in the abnormal, in the ill. And slowly, because all that he studied was nothing but illness, he started feeling that there is no hope for man.

To study illness is needed, because ill people have to be helped. But they cannot be really helped unless you know what wellness is. At the most, you can make people adjusted to the society, but the society itself is ill.

That's what modern psychotherapies go on doing. Whenever somebody becomes a little maladjusted, the work of the psychiatrist is to pull him back to adjustment. Adjustment is thought to be normal. But that is not necessarily the case – because if the society itself is abnormal then to get adjusted to it will be abnormality, not normality.

In fact, people like R D Laing have become suspicious of the whole project. The society is abnormal, and you help people to be adjusted to it? You serve the society, you don't serve those people. You are agents of the society, of the status quo, of the establishment. The person whom you are treating – through drugs, through shock treatments, through psychoanalysis and a thousand and one other methods – may be really a normal person, and because he is normal he cannot adjust to the abnormal society.

Just think of a buddha – a buddha cannot adjust to the society. The buddhas have always been rebellious. They cannot bow down to the society, they cannot surrender to the society – the society is ill! The society has been living under a curse, the curse that has been created by the priests and the politicians. It has been living under a great conspiracy. People have not been allowed to be healthy, because healthy people are dangerous. People are not allowed to be intelligent, because intelligent people are dangerous.

Your educational system exists not to help people to become intelligent, but to hinder people from becoming intelligent. It exists so that everybody can be reduced to a mediocre being, so that everybody is reduced to a stupid scholar. And 25 years of conditioning from kindergarten to the university can reduce anybody to a stupid scholar, can make anybody mediocre – because your education requires that people should be able to reproduce whatsoever has been taught to them. That is the criterion to judge their intelligence.

That may be the criterion to judge their parrot-like memory, but it is not the criterion of their intelligence. Intelligence is a totally different phenomenon. Intelligence has nothing to do with repetition; in fact intelligence will abhor repetition. Intelligence will always try to live life in its own way. Intelligence will want to do its own thing. Intelligence will want to enter into life's mysteries, not according to set formulas or prescribed strategies. Intelligence is always original.

Universities don't allow original people to exist. They weed out original people; their whole effort is to destroy originality because original people will always create trouble in the society. They will not be so easily manipulated, and they cannot be so easily reduced to clerks and schoolteachers – they cannot be so easily reduced to efficient machines. They will assert themselves; they will try to live life not according to a pattern but according to their own insight.

If a person loves music, even if he has to remain a beggar he will persist in living the life of a musician. Even if he has the choice of becoming the prime minister he would rather live like a beggar and go on playing his music. That will be intelligence, because only when you live your life according to your own light, according to your own insights, according to your own inner voice, do you attain to bliss, to fulfilment.

To become a prime minister you don't need intelligence. In fact if you have intelligence you cannot become a prime minister, because who would like to go into politics if he has intelligence? Who would like to go into that ugly game? One would like to become a poet or a painter or a dancer, but who would like to become a politician? Not the intelligent person but only those who are still barbarians, only those who still enjoy violence and domination over other people.

Universities destroy intelligence. Your education is very destructive to intelligence – it serves the society, and the society is abnormal, very abnormal. In three thousand years, five thousand wars have been fought – can you say this society is healthy? Can you say this society is sane? Man is always ready to kill, murder or commit suicide. What kind of society is this?

Psychiatry and psychoanalysis try to adjust people. They call unadjusted people "abnormal". That's why psychologists go on saying that Jesus was abnormal. In fact, they say he was neurotic. Jesus neurotic! And the people who managed to murder this man, they were healthy? Jesus is neurotic and Pontius Pilate is healthy, normal.

If Jesus is neurotic, then Buddha is neurotic, Mahavira is neurotic, Pythagoras, Patanjali, Lao Tzu, Zarathustra, all are neurotics. Socrates is neurotic – and the judges who decided that he should be poisoned and killed, they are normal.

The whole earth is a madhouse. Who is ill? And how can you decide and define illness unless you know what wellness is?

Sigmund Freud missed, because he only studied ill people. Ill people can be studied, because illness always happens on the periphery. Well people cannot be studied, because wellness happens at the centre; it wells up in your being. Illness is superficial, wellness is intrinsic. Sigmund Freud cannot study a buddha, because he will not be able to find any symptoms.

You can go to a doctor and you can ask, "What is the definition of health?" and you will be surprised that no doctor can answer it. At the most he can say, "When a person is not ill, he is healthy." What kind of definition is this? "When a person has no illnesses he is healthy." Health is a positive phenomenon and you are defining it negatively.

Illness they can define; they can define what is cancer and what is tuberculosis and they can define all kinds of illnesses – millions of illnesses they can define. But a single phenomenon, health, remains indefinable – it has not been studied at all.

Unless psychology becomes rooted in people who are whole and holy – who are enlightened, alert, aware, who have transcended all kinds of identifications, who have become pure consciousness – unless psychology studies these people . . . But then psychology will have to change its methods. Then it cannot go on imitating physiology, physics, chemistry and the natural sciences. Then it will have to learn much from literature, from poetry, from music. Then it will have to move closer to the arts rather than following science.

It has been a misfortune that Sigmund Freud was basically a physician, a medical doctor. His idea of making a science of psychology was the idea of medical science. He started studying ill people, and he based his whole understanding in the illnesses. And when you treat ill people, only ill people come to you – slowly, all you know about man is that which you have known through ill people. Then that becomes your understanding about human beings. That's why whatever Freud says about man is basically wrong. It is about the ill person – it is not about the human being, it is not about humanity. It is not about a real human being, it is something about an ill person.

For example, if you study only blind people, and you decide that no person can see, what kind of understanding will that be? It will not be true about human beings as such, it will only be true about blind people.

Psychiatrists only come across ill people and then they start deciding about humanity, they start defining mankind. That is going beyond their limits. First you will have to understand the whole – the ill and the well person both. In fact, the person who is perfectly well should be the criterion; he should be the decisive factor.

Psychology has to become the psychology of the buddhas. Only then will it be true, authentic.

My effort is not that of a psychiatrist or a psychotherapist. I am not treating ill people. My effort is to release the sources of well-being in you. I am not interested in treating you, I am interested in freeing you.

You ask: is there any particular method of meditation useful for treatment of a particular type of mental illness? No. That does not mean that meditation cannot help – it helps, but that is coincidental. It helps, but that is only a by-product.

My basic effort is to create buddhas – people who are whole. I am not treating ill people – although a few ill people come, and they are helped, that is not my purpose here. It is not a therapeutic community, it is a spiritual commune. Therapies are happening here, but they are not basically meant for ill people because in my vision the whole of humanity is ill, it is abnormal.

The therapies that happen here are not particularly interested in any particular kind of disease. We are simply helping so-called normal people to become *really* normal.

As I see it, every human being is brought up by ill people, abnormal people – the parents, the teachers – and naturally they go on giving their illnesses to their children. Unless one becomes alert about what has been done to oneself, unless one dares, is courageous, has guts to drop all conditioning, one never becomes normal.

Many therapeutic groups are run here just to help common people, the so-called normal people; be aware that they are not normal – that is the first step toward becoming normal. Once you have understood that you are not normal, things start changing. A great awareness starts arising in you: something has to be done, something becomes urgent.

We help people to drop their conditionings – Hindu, Christian, Mohammedan, communist, we help people to drop *all* their conditionings, because only an unconditioned being is really normal and natural. Conditionings are perversions.

So we are not really interested in helping so-called ill people, our work is to help the so-called normal people. But sometimes ill people come and they are benefited. That is just a fringe phenomenon, on the margin.

I cannot say which meditation is going to help which particular disease. In fact, each meditation will help in some way or other, because all meditation techniques are basically moving to the same point of inner silence. The method may be active or the method may be passive, it doesn't matter; the goal is the same. It may be a Sufi method, it may be a Zen method – the goal is the same. The goal is to make you so silent that all thinking disappears and you are just a mirror, reflecting that which is.

My definition of "God" is that which is, and once you start seeing that which is and you start falling in tune with it, well-being arises. You become part of this tremendously beautiful universe.

Psychoanalysis and psychiatry help ill people. Meditation helps people who are already well but would like to know the peaks of wellness – would like to go to the Everest of wellness, what Abraham Maslow calls "peak experiences". Those peak experiences are everybody's birthright. If you don't have peak experiences you are missing something immensely valuable.

But meditation goes even one step further than Abraham Maslow and humanistic psychologies. It is not only a question of attaining peak experiences – because peak experiences will come and go; you cannot remain on the peak forever. You can have a deep orgasmic experience, you can attain to a peak, but the moment you have attained you have already started going downhill. You cannot stay on the peak; there is no space to stay.

All peaks are the repetition of the ancient myth of Sisyphus. Sisyphus was punished by the gods because he rebelled against them. He has to push a rock to the peak of a mountain, but the peak is small and the rock is big; the moment the rock reaches the peak it starts falling back, slipping back downhill.

That is the story of every human being. You cannot stay on the peak. You will make the journey, the long journey, to reach the peak – and once you have attained, it is finished. The moment you become aware of reaching the peak, it is no more; you have started going downhill. There is no space to abide there.

Meditation helps you not only to attain peak experiences, beautiful experiences – that is only for the beginners – but to have a total, orgasmic consciousness. Not the peak experience, not the orgasmic experience, but an orgasmic consciousness so that you are 24 hours in an orgasmic ecstasy. So that your whole life, moment to moment, is a celebration.

My effort is that of meditation, of religiousness. I help people first to know peak experiences so that a great longing can arise in them to abide on those peaks. But one cannot abide on those peaks. Then another effort starts in your life, to create orgasmic *consciousness*. Peaks are experiences; they come and go. Orgasmic consciousness is a transformation of your being. It is a new birth, a resurrection. Attaining to peak experiences helps many ill people. I am not concerned with it, but it helps.

I'd like to know how the use of therapy in your work differs from other therapies like the Freudian psychoanalytic approach, the humanistic and growth groups.

It is fundamentally different from any other therapy that has existed. The most fundamental difference is that all those therapies are for sick people, those who are mentally not well. Those therapies make an effort to bring them back to their normal life. All those therapies serve the needs of society. The society drives people mad, crazy, schizophrenic. The therapies bring them back into their normal, average mind so they can function again in the old pattern where they had become incapable of functioning.

All the therapies – Freudian or Jungian or Adlerian – their function is the same as was the function of the priest in the past. These are the priests of a sophisticated time, but their function is the same. It is against revolution, against change.

Why does this society go on creating sick people? No animal is sick in that way. Why does human society go on creating schizophrenic people? Why there are so many rapes, why there are so many people burdened with guilt, why there are so many murders, suicides? And even though a person somehow manages to live normally, deep down nobody is normal. They all have nightmares, they all have fear, they all have greed, they all feel insecure. These therapies are in the service of the society that drives people nuts.

The basic difference is that I am trying to help people understand that they are not responsible for their mental sickness; they are victims. My purpose is not to make then normal so that they can go back to church and back to the office and back to the same wife and the same world. No, my function is to give people a fresh individuality, a rebellious intelligence, a perspective in which they can see that the society has manipulated and exploited them, almost killed them.

This is the first part of therapy as it is used in my work: that the person should be made aware that it is the society that is sick and he is only a victim.

Second, we make the person aware that he is a victim because he is more intelligent than other people. Idiots don't go crazy, they do have not the capacity to go crazy. To have a sick mind, first you need to have a mind. Normal and average people who are thought to be mentally healthy are really intellectually retarded; even if they want to go mad they cannot. Madness needs some intelligence.

It is not a coincidence that so many of the great painters, poets, scientists, musicians – people who have touched in some dimension the highest peak of intelligence – go mad. Many of them commit suicide. Strange . . . we have created really a strange world where idiots are normal and geniuses are abnormal, where idiots don't go mad but geniuses do, and suffer all kinds of mental torture. The old therapies try to bring them back, to force them back to the ordinary, retarded humanity.

Of course these people are a minority, so naturally they think something is wrong with them. Among millions of people who are retarded, to be intelligent is really unsafe. It is insecure, it is dangerous. Where people are living below the mental age of 13 – that is the average mental age of the masses – to have more intelligence is going to create trouble for you. They are "the society" and you are just an individual, helpless.

My effort is to make these people aware that their sickness is significant. They need not feel embarrassed, they should really rejoice because they have intelligence – enough intelligence, more intelligence than the ordinary normal people. That's why they are having trouble. They cannot adjust with the society; they feel everywhere a misfit. That's what gives people the idea that something is wrong with them. The reality is just the opposite. They are the right people, but they are in very small minority. And the majority is stupid, but it is majority. Your so-called therapists are simply serving the vested interests.

My effort is to give you a confidence that your sickness is symbolic, that you don't have a defective mind, that you should not feel bad about it. In fact, you should feel grateful to existence because you have raised questions that ordinary people don't raise. You have created problems in your life that ordinary people don't create. And because you were not fitting with the majority, the masses, the crowd, they have denounced you as mad.

The Freudians and the Jungians and the Adlerians all accept that idea that you are mad and need treatment. And their whole treatment is bringing you down to the lowest denominator in society. My effort is just the opposite: first to make you feel relaxed about your situation, help you recognize that the society is sick, not you, that the society needs a change and a revolution, not you. If you are not fitting with the society, the reason is not that you are mad. The reason is that you have so much intelligence that you cannot fit with all these retarded people.

Second, which is even more important, the therapy in my work helps you first to regain your confidence, your self-respect, the understanding that nothing is wrong with you. But this is only the groundwork. *Then* the real work starts. Everybody around you has forced you to believe that something is wrong with you – first we have to clean all that nonsense and make you self-respectful. Then begins the real work of meditation.

Therapy is only preparing the ground. It is not enough. It is just to undo what the society has done to you. Once it is undone, once you are unburdened, then begins the real work: the exploration into your own interiority. So therapy, according to me, is only the groundwork for creating space and the urge to explore your reality.

All those therapists, psychoanalysts, psychiatrists – they have nothing to do with meditation. They are not there to help you to grow. In fact, they are there to cut as many branches from you as possible – your height, your growth – so you become similar to other pygmies. And because you accept the ideas of the common mass, you allow them to cut your intelligence, to destroy your questioning, to hinder any possibility of going deeper than ordinary people. My work is first to unburden you and then to give you the vision, the perception that this is not the end. Just not to be sick cannot be the end. Just not to be sick is not enough. You have to be psychologically healthy, whole. And unless you come to self-realization, the work is unfinished.

Therapy stops at the point where you have become again normal, you have been dragged back. My work respects your sickness, because it reflects the whole society. You became a victim of it because you were more vulnerable, more open, more available. You have been wounded from every side. You were more innocent, and you were intelligent enough not to

209

participate in superstitions and idiotic ideologies. All this has brought you condemnation.

Religions used to send you to hell. Now they have become outdated and nobody bothers much about hell. In fact, nobody believes in it. Now you are being sent to the couch of the psychoanalyst, which is a constant torture for years and years. In fact, there is not a single human being who has been totally psychoanalysed. A strange kind of science you have!

It takes seven years, nine years, ten years and still you are not fully analysed. Still the problems are there. Perhaps you have become more accepting of them, perhaps you have become aware not to express them in the society, not to behave in such a way that people think you are strange. They have taught you how to adjust, and that takes years and thousands of dollars – just to be adjusted to idiots!

My effort is to give you back your individuality. It is your individuality that has rebelled against the social norms, and it is your individuality that has refused to be destroyed. My function is to help you discover your whole, revolutionary individuality, your uniqueness. I am not here to make you a cog in the wheel of this big civilization and culture that we have been creating for millions of years. We have ended in making the whole earth a madhouse.

There is a story by Kahlil Gibran. One of his friends goes mad. He could not believe it, because that man was so intelligent, and he has been put into a madhouse? Gibran goes to meet him. He is feeling very sad and sorry for him.

The friend was sitting on a bench under a tree in the garden of that madhouse. Gibran approached him, and wanted to show his sympathy. The man started laughing. Gibran said, "So it seems you have really gone mad. I am showing sympathy, compassion, my friendship, and you are laughing."

The man said, "I have to laugh, because those people who are mad just because they are in the majority cannot convince me that I am mad. In fact, since I have been in the madhouse I am immensely happy because I left the madhouse out there. Here I can live as sanely as I want. Nobody will interfere.

"You should not feel sorry for me – in fact, I feel sorry for you. What the hell are you doing in that great madhouse outside? Why don't you come here and live with me?"

Kahlil Gibran was shocked, but a great question arose in his mind. Perhaps that man was right.

To me, there is no perhaps. That man is right.

So therapy as it is used in my work is a search for your individuality and its uniqueness. Then, once you are freed from the idea that you are sick, there opens a new dimension. Then you can grow into being more conscious, and ultimately enlightened. I use your sickness for your ultimate health, wholeness. About that wholeness your therapists are completely unaware. They are unaware even what they are doing. They are simply serving the politicians, the religions, the vested interests, they are not helping you. They are part of the status quo.

The therapists who work with me are not part of status quo. They are basically people who are helping you to get rid of all those ideas that people have forced into your mind, that something is wrong with you. Once you are completely free of that garbage, meditation becomes simple, very spontaneous. You drop out of the rotten society and you are available to the whole existence. Once you start getting roots and becoming centred, meditations are very easy. And they can lead you to the ultimate experience of life.

Those normal people never achieve that experience. They don't have even the intelligence to become sick! It is just like a dead man cannot fall sick. A dead man is always healthy, there is no way to make him sick. Even if you inject him with poison, there is no way to make him sick; he will remain perfectly healthy.

It is life that is fragile and can be easily made sick, destroyed. Intelligence is even more fragile. If life is a tree, then intelligence is the flower – even more fragile. More colourful, more alive, more expressive, more poetic – but more fragile. And enlightenment is the ultimate in fragility. It is just like the fragrance; you cannot even catch hold of it. You can feel its presence, you can smell its existence, but there is no way to have it in your fist.

So my use of therapy is fundamentally different. Its purpose is different, its approach is different. The other therapies respect the society and condemn the individual. I respect the individual and I condemn the mob, because the mass of people has no soul in it. It is just a big crowd of almost dead people who don't know what life is and who will never know what life is.

So therapies are the groundwork, and then meditation. Once a deep acceptance has come to you, then you can grow.

Research has suggested that certain states of consciousness brought about by meditation techniques appear to evoke specific brainwave patterns. These states are now being created by electronic and auditory stimulation of the brain, and they can be learned through biofeedback.

The traditional 'meditative state' – sitting silently (or at least quietly alert) is composed of bilateral, synchronous alpha waves. Deeper meditation also has bilateral theta waves. A state called 'lucid awareness' has the bilateral synchronous alpha and theta waves of deep meditation, plus the beta waves of normal thought processes. 'Lucid awareness' can be learned through biofeedback, using the most modern equipment.

Are these kinds of stimulation and biofeedback useful tools for the meditator? What is the relationship of these technological techniques to the meditation beyond technique? Is this an example of bringing science together with meditation?

It is a very complex question. You will have to understand one of the most fundamental things about meditation – that no technique leads to meditation. The old so-called techniques and the new scientific biofeedback techniques are the same as far as meditation is concerned.

Meditation is not a by-product of any technique. Meditation happens beyond mind. No technique can go beyond mind. But there is going to be a great misunderstanding in scientific circles, and it has a certain basis. The basis of all misunderstanding is: when the being of a person is in a state of meditation, it creates certain waves in the mind. These waves can be created from the outside by technical means. But those waves will not create meditation – this is the misunderstanding.

Meditation creates those waves; it is the mind reflecting the inner world.

You cannot see what is happening inside. But you can see what is happening in the mind. Now there are sensitive instruments . . . we can judge what kind of waves are there when a person is asleep, what kinds of waves are there when a person is dreaming, what kinds of waves are there when a person is in meditation.

But by creating the waves, you cannot create the situation – because those waves are only symptoms, indicators.

It is perfectly good, you can study them. But remember that there is no shortcut to meditation, and no mechanical device can be of any help. In fact, meditation needs no technique – scientific or otherwise.

Meditation is simply an understanding.

It is not a question of sitting silently, it is not a question of chanting a mantra. It is a question of understanding the subtle workings of the mind. As you understand those workings of the mind a great awareness arises in you which is not of the mind. That awareness arises in your being, in your soul, in your consciousness.

Mind is only a mechanism, but when that awareness arises it is bound to create a certain energy pattern around it. That energy pattern is noted by the mind. Mind is a very subtle mechanism.

And you are studying from the outside, so at the most you can study the mind. Seeing that whenever a person is silent, serene, peaceful, a certain wave pattern always, inevitably appears in the mind, the scientific thinking will say: if we can create this wave pattern in the mind, through some biofeedback technology, then the being inside will reach the heights of awareness.

This is not going to happen. It is not a question of cause and effect. These waves in the mind are not the cause of meditation; they are, on the contrary, the effect. From the effect you cannot move toward the cause.

It is possible that with biofeedback you can learn to create certain patterns in the mind and they will give a feeling of peace, silence and serenity to the person. Because the person himself does not know what meditation is, and has no way of comparing, he may be misled into believing that this is meditation – but it is not. Because the moment the

214

biofeedback mechanism stops, the waves disappear, and the silence and the peace and the serenity also disappear. And you may go on practicing with those scientific instruments for years; it will not change your character, it will not change your morality, it will not change your individuality. You will remain the same.

Meditation transforms. It takes you to higher levels of consciousness and changes your whole lifestyle. It changes your reactions into responses to such an extent that it is unbelievable that the person who would have reacted in the same situation in anger is now acting in deep compassion, with love – in the same situation.

Meditation is a state of being, arrived at through understanding. It needs intelligence, it does not need techniques. There is no technique that can give you intelligence. Otherwise, we would have changed all the idiots into geniuses; all the mediocre people would have become Albert Einsteins, Bertrand Russells, Jean-Paul Sartres. There is no way to change your intelligence from the outside, to sharpen it, to make it more penetrating, to give it more insight. It is simply a question of understanding, and nobody else can do it for you – no machine, no man.

For centuries the so-called gurus have been cheating humanity. In the future, instead of gurus, these guru machines will cheat humanity.

The gurus were cheating people, saying that "We will give you a mantra. You repeat the mantra." Certainly by repeating a mantra continuously, you create the energy field of a certain wavelength; but the man remains the same, because it is only on the surface. It is just as if you have thrown a pebble into the silent lake and ripples arise and move all over the lake from one corner to the other corner, but it does not touch the depths of the lake at all. The depths are completely unaware of what is happening on the surface.

And what you see on the surface is also illusory. You think that ripples are moving – that's not true. Nothing is moving.

When you throw a pebble into the lake, it is not that ripples start moving. You can check it by putting a small flower on the water. You will be surprised: the flower remains in the same place. If the waves were moving and going toward the shore, they would have taken the flower with them. The flower remains there. The waves are not moving; it is just the water going up and down in the same place, creating the illusion of movement. The depths of the lake will not know anything about it. And there is going to be no change in the character, in the beauty of the lake by creating those waves.

Mind is between the world and you.

Whatever happens in the world, the mind is affected by it; and you can understand through the mind what is happening outside.

For example, you are looking at me – you cannot see *me*; it is your mind that is affected by certain rays and creates a picture in the mind. You are inside, and from inside you see the picture. You don't see me; you can't see me. The mind is the mediator. Just as when the inner consciousness is affected by the outside, can read what is happening outside, what the scientists are trying to do is just the same: they are studying meditators and reading their wavelengths, the energy fields created by meditation. And naturally, the scientific approach is that if these certain patterns appear without any exception when a person is in meditation, then we have got the key; if we can create these patterns in the mind, then meditation is bound to appear inside.

That's where the fallacy is.

You can create the pattern in the mind, and if the person does not know about meditation, he may feel a silence, a serenity – for the moment, as long as those waves remain. But you cannot deceive a meditator because the meditator will see that those patterns are appearing in the mind . . .

Mind is a lower reality, and the lower reality cannot change the higher reality. The mind is the servant; it cannot change the master.

But you can experiment. Just remain aware that whether it is a biofeedback machine or a chanting of OM, it does not matter; it only creates a mental peace, and a mental peace is not meditation.

Meditation is the flight beyond the mind. It has nothing to do with mental peace.

An American thinker, Joshua Liebman, has written a very famous book, *Peace of Mind*. I wrote him a letter many years ago when I came across the book, saying that "If you are sincere and honest, you should withdraw the book from the market because there is no such thing as peace of mind. Mind is the problem. When there is no mind then there is peace, so how there can be peace of mind? And any peace of mind is only fallacious; it simply means that the noise has slowed down to such a point that you think it is silence. And you don't have anything to compare it with."

A man who knows what meditation is cannot be deceived by any techniques, because no technique can give you understanding of the workings of the mind.

For example, you feel anger, you feel jealousy, you feel hatred, you feel lust. Is there any technique that can help you to get rid of anger? Of jealousy? Of hatred? Of sexual lust? And if these things continue to remain, your lifestyle is going to remain the same as before.

There is only one way – there has never been a second. There is one and only one way to understand that to be angry is to be stupid: watch anger in all its phases, be alert to it so it does not catch you unawares; remain watchful, seeing every step of the anger. And you will be surprised: as awareness about the ways of anger grows, the anger starts evaporating.

And when the anger disappears, then there is a peace. Peace is not a positive achievement. When the hatred disappears, there is love. Love is not a positive achievement. When jealousy disappears, there is a deep friendliness toward all.

Try to understand . . .

But all the religions have corrupted your minds because they have not taught you how to watch, how to understand; instead they have given you conclusions – that anger is bad. And the moment you condemn something, you have already taken a certain position of judgement. You have judged. Now you cannot be aware.

Awareness needs a state of no-judgement.

And all the religions have been teaching people judgements: this is good, this is bad, this is sin, this is virtue – this is the whole crap that for centuries man's mind has been loaded with. So, with everything – the moment you see it – there is immediately a judgement about it within you. You cannot simply see it, you cannot be just a mirror without saying anything.

Understanding arises by becoming a mirror, a mirror of all that goes on in the mind.

There is a beautiful story – not just a story, but an actual historical fact.

A disciple of Gautam Buddha was going on a journey to spread his message. He had come to see Gautam Buddha and to get his blessings, and to ask if there was any last message, any last words to be said to him.

And Gautam Buddha said, "Just remember one thing: while walking, keep your gaze just four feet ahead, looking four feet ahead of you."

Since that day, for 25 centuries, Buddhist monks have walked in the same way. That was a strategy to keep the monks from seeing women in particular. Those disciples were monks. They had taken the vow of celibacy.

Ananda, another of Gautam Buddha's disciples, could not understand what the matter was, why the monk should keep his eyes always focused four feet ahead. He enquired: "I want to know, what is the matter?"

Buddha said, "That's how he will avoid looking at a woman, at least a woman's face – at the most he will see her feet."

But Ananda said, "There may be situations when a woman is in danger. For example, she has fallen into a well and is shouting for help. What is your disciple supposed to do? He will have to see her face, her body."

Buddha said, "In special situations he is allowed to see her, but it is not the rule, it is only the exception."

Ananda said, "What about touching? Because there may be situations when a woman has fallen on the road. What is your disciple supposed to do? Should he help her to get up or not? Or an old woman wants to cross the road – what is your disciple supposed to do?"

Buddha said, "As an exception – but remember it is not a rule – he can touch the woman with one condition, and if he cannot fulfil the condition he is not allowed the exceptions. The condition is that he should remain just a mirror, he should not take any judgement, any attitude. 'The woman is beautiful' – that is a judgement. 'The woman is fair' – that is a judgement. He should remain a mirror, then he is allowed the exceptions. Otherwise, let the woman drown in the well – somebody else will save her. You save yourself!"

What he is saying is this: in every situation where mind starts any kind of desire, greed, lust, ambition, possessiveness, the meditator has to be just a mirror. And what is that going to do? To be just a mirror means you are simply aware.

In pure awareness the mind cannot drag you down into the mud, into the gutter. In anger, in hatred, in jealousy, the mind is absolutely impotent in the face of awareness. And because the mind is absolutely impotent, your whole being is in a profound silence – the peace that passeth understanding.

Naturally that peace, that silence, that joy, that blissfulness will affect the mind. It will create ripples in the mind, it will change the wavelengths in the mind, and the scientist will be reading those waves, those wave patterns, and he will be thinking, "If these wave patterns can be created in someone by mechanical devices, then we will be able to create the profoundness of a Gautam Buddha."

Don't be stupid.

All your technical devices can be good, can be helpful. They are not going to do any harm; they will be giving some taste of peace, of silence – although very superficial, still it is something for those who have never known anything of peace.

For the thirsty, even dirty water does not look dirty.

For the thirsty, even dirty water is a great blessing.

So you can start your experiments with all my blessings, but remember it is not meditation that you are giving to people – you don't know meditation yourself. You may be giving them a little rest, a little relaxation – and there is nothing wrong in it.

But if you give them the idea that this is meditation then you are certainly being harmful – because these people will stop at the technical things, with the superficial silence, thinking that this is all and they have gained it.

You can be helpful to people. Tell them that "This is just a mechanical way of putting your mind at peace, and mind at peace is not the real peace – real peace is when mind is absent. And that is not possible from the outside, but only from the inside. And inside you have the intelligence, the understanding to do the miracle."

It is good for people who cannot relax, who cannot find a few moments of peace, whose minds are continuously chattering – your technical devices are good, your biofeedback mechanisms are good. But make it clear to them that this is not meditation, this is just a mechanical device to help you relax, to give you a superficial feeling of silence. If this silence creates an urge in you to find the real, the inner, the authentic source of peace, then those technical devices have been friends, and the technicians who have been using them have not been barriers but have been bridges. Become a bridge.

Give people the little taste that is possible through machines, but don't give them the false idea that this is what meditation is. Tell them that this is only a faraway echo of the real; if you want the real, you will have to go through a deep inner search, a profound understanding of your mind, an awareness of all the cunning ways of the mind so that the mind can be put aside. Then the mind is no longer between you and existence, and the doors are open.

Meditation is the ultimate experience of blissfulness.

It cannot be produced by drugs, it cannot be produced by machines, it cannot be produced from the outside.

Forget About Enlightenment

Enlightenment is a by-product of the understanding that to live in the past is foolish, because it is simply memory. But millions of people are wasting their time in memories. Millions of others are living in the future. You cannot live in the future; it is making castles in the air.

To understand that past and future are both non-existential . . . all that you have got is a very small moment: this very moment. You don't even get two moments together. When one moment is gone, you get another moment. You always have only one moment in your hands; and it is so small and so fleeting, that if you are thinking of the past and the future, you will miss it. And that is the only life and the only reality there is.

Understanding this whole process, one thing becomes certain: why the mind avoids the present, which is the real, and why it tries to get involved with past and future, which are not real. As one tries to understand that, one thing becomes clear: that in the present moment, mind cannot exist.

Mind is simply a collection of memories of the past, and – out of those memories – imagination about the future.

Mind does not know three tenses. It knows only two: past and future. Present is non-existential to the mind. The existential is non-existential to the mind; and the non-

222

existentials are existential to the mind. Hence the whole effort is how to get out of the mind, how to get out of the non-existentials and to stand in the middle – where existence is.

How to be in the present? That is the whole knack of meditation. And the moment you are in the present, enlightenment is its by-product. Don't give it to the mind – the mind will immediately make it a goal. Mind cannot do anything else. It cannot put it in the past because you have never experienced it, so the past is closed. You have yet to experience it; naturally, it has to be put somewhere in the future. And it always happens in the present.

So forget about enlightenment. It is a by-product; you cannot do anything about it. This is the beauty of by-products: you have to do something else, and the by-product comes in. You have to learn to be in the present more and more. In other words: you have to learn to be in a state of no-mind more and more.

It was for a certain reason that mystics called meditation "no-mind": if you call it meditation, again the mind makes a goal out of it. Then you have to achieve meditation. So it makes no difference whether the goal is enlightenment or meditation: the goal remains, the future remains, and goes on destroying the present.

The mystics who changed from "meditation" to "no-mind" had a tremendous insight. Now no-mind cannot be made a goal: mind cannot make it a goal. It is simply absurd – how can mind make a goal of no-mind? It will simply say it is not possible; mind is all, there is no no-mind.

This was a strategy not to allow you to make it a goal. Very few people have understood the strategy: that that's why they have called it no-mind – to prevent the mind from making it a goal.

So be more and more in a state of no-mind. Just go on removing memories, imagination, to clean and clear the present moment. And as it deepens, as you become more and more capable of no-mind, enlightenment comes of its own accord.

Enlightenment is simply recognizing your being, recognizing the eternity of your being, recognizing that there has been no death before, nor is there any death to come – that death is a fiction. Seeing your being in its utter nakedness, in its absolute beauty, its grandeur, its silence, its blissfulness, its ecstasy – all that is involved in the word "enlightenment".

Once you have experienced that juice, mind starts losing its grip on you because you have found something which is qualitatively so high, so fulfilling, such a tremendous contentment, that mind feels its function is finished. It looks ugly, because it has only given you misery, worries, anxiety. What has been its contribution to you? Its grip loosens; it starts hiding in the shadows, and by and by it falls away.

You continue to live, but now your living is moment to moment; and what you have got as a by-product in that small gap of no-mind goes on growing. There is no end to that growth.

Enlightenment only begins, it never ends.

Nobody has said this before. They have all said that it is perfect – but perfection means it cannot grow. It has happened once, and all growth, all evolution, is finished.

But as far as my experience is concerned, I can say very authoritatively that anything that you are stuck with permanently cannot remain ecstatic, cannot remain blissful. You will start taking it for granted.

It was ecstatic because you had lived in agony; compared to that agony it was ecstatic. You have lived in pain, in wounds;

against that, it was contentment, fulfilment. But now, day after day, month after month, year after year, life after life, you have forgotten agony, the taste of pain. And with that forgetfulness, your enlightenment will become just ordinary – something that you take for granted, dull and dead. The ecstasy is the same but you cannot feel it the same. There has come a full stop, and life knows no full stop.

But why have all these mystics insisted that it is perfect? Because they were afraid. Logically they were not able to face the philosophers, the critics . . . because if you say it is imperfect, that means something more has to happen. You have not attained the goal – something is still missing. So it is partial, what you have attained. If it is not perfect, it is partial.

To avoid calling it partial, they said that it is perfect. But they forgot that someday somebody can raise a question against perfection. It has not been raised yet, but I am raising it: perfection is going to be dead, it cannot be living, because nothing is going to happen. It will be the same tomorrow and the day after tomorrow, for eternity.

You will get utterly bored with your ecstasy, with your contentment, and there is no going back. You cannot find that agony again, those moments of misery again, because all that has fallen out of your being. There is no way back, and in the future, for as far as you can see, it will remain the same.

I deny perfection. Enlightenment appears perfect because nothing seems to be missing at the moment. All that you have ever dreamt – it is much more than that. All that you could have ever conceived – it is much more than that. So it appears absolute, perfect, ultimate; but this is a fallacy. It will grow, it will become vast. New qualities will be added to it; and each time it is going to be a surprise because you have never thought about this quality.

So I want it to be clearly understood by my people that enlightenment is only a beginning, the beginning of tremendous evolution that has no limits. Only then can you remain dancing, singing. And you can remain thrilled every moment, because one never knows what the next moment is going to bring – new insights, new visions, new experiences.

And there is no limitation to it. There never comes a point when you can say the journey has ended. The journey only begins, it never ends.

Other mystics have not said it because they were afraid that if you say to people that the journey only begins and never ends, they will never begin it. What is the point of a journey that begins and never ends? Then do something else. Why waste your life in such a journey, where nowhere will you find a place where you can say, "I have come home"?

But I want to be absolutely truthful about enlightenment. And I want it to be an excitement that it does not end. It is not something against it, it is something favourable about it – that everything goes on expanding, everything goes on growing, everything goes on getting higher; and still the infinite sky is there, the infinite universe is there.

And if the universe can be infinite ... which is inconceivable for the mind; you cannot conceive the universe as infinite. Mind cannot conceive infinity, for the simple reason that mind functions through logic. It will say, "It may be far away, but somewhere it has to end. How can it go on and on and on? We may never reach the end, we may never find the boundary line where the universe ends – that is possible because we are limited – but that does not mean that the universe is unlimited."

Logic cannot conceive it, thinking cannot have any justification for it. And if you start thinking, you cannot believe it. You can push on the boundary as far as you can but the boundary remains.

But the truth is, the boundary cannot be there, because a boundary always needs two things: one on this side and one on the other side. You cannot make a boundary with only one side. You have a fence around your house because there is a neighbor's house. Your fence is not the end – it is simply the beginning of another house.

So if sometime logic forces you to conclude there must be a boundary, it has to be asked: what will be beyond the boundary? There must be something. Even though it is going to be nothing, that nothing will also be part of the universe. Why are you creating a boundary? That emptiness will also be the universe.

Once you understand that every boundary needs two things – something that it closes and something that it opens – then you can have some idea that a finite universe is impossible. Only an infinite universe is possible.

But for the infinite universe you need an infinity of growth, because if you come to a point where you think you have become perfect, you fall out of tune with the universe.

The same logic has to be understood about evolution. It has to be forever and forever – because again there is the question of a boundary.

You cannot make any boundaries in existence.

Boundaries do not belong to reality.

One of my professors, Doctor S S Roy, had written a doctoral thesis on Bradley and Shankara – both are absolutists, both believe in perfection. And his doctoral thesis was accepted, he got the PhD.

But I told him, "You may have got the PhD, but if I had been one of the examiners of your thesis, you would not have got it, because Shankara and Bradley are preaching – and you are trying to make a comparative study, that they are saying the same thing – that there is a boundary at perfection. And you are saying it with so much emphasis that it seems you also believe in it."

He said, "Yes, I have been studying Shankara and Bradley my whole life, and they have left an immense impact on me. They both are the greatest philosophers in the world."

But I said, "They are just childish, that both believe there is a boundary at perfection. Then there is no growth possible. Perfection is death and life is growth."

And I asked him directly, "Would you like to be perfect and dead, or imperfect and alive? That is the choice."

He said, "I have never thought about it – that perfection means death, and imperfection means growth. But when you say it, it sounds correct."

And I said, "You just think: for how long has existence been there? It has not yet reached perfection. Growth has not stopped, evolution has not stopped, and existence has been for eternity. So what reason can there be to think that tomorrow it will be perfect?

"The whole of eternity in the past has failed to make it perfect. What reason is there to think that just one day more is needed, or a few days, or a few years? We are always in the middle." I told him, "We are always in the middle. We will never know the beginning because there has never been one, and we will never know the end because there is not going to be any."

We are always in the middle, growing. It is eternal growth, in all the dimensions.

And the same applies to enlightenment.

228

How does watching lead to no-mind? I am more and more able to watch my body, my thoughts and feelings and this feels beautiful. But moments of no thoughts are few and far between. When I hear you saying "meditation is witnessing", I feel I understand. But when you talk about no-mind, it doesn't sound easy at all. Would you please comment?

Meditation covers a very long pilgrimage. When I say meditation is witnessing, it is the beginning of meditation. And when I say meditation is no-mind, it is the completion of the pilgrimage. Witnessing is the beginning, and no-mind is the fulfilment. Witnessing is the method to reach the no-mind. Naturally you will feel witnessing is easier. It is closer to you.

But witnessing is only like planting seeds, and then is the long waiting period. Not only waiting, but trusting that this seed is going to sprout, that it is going to become a bush; that one day the spring will come and the bush will have flowers. No-mind is the last stage of flowering.

Sowing the seed is of course very easy; it is within your hands. But bringing the flowers is beyond you. You can prepare the whole ground, but the flowers will come on their own accord; you cannot manage to force them to come. The spring is beyond your reach – but if your preparation is perfect, spring comes; that is absolutely guaranteed.

It is perfectly good, the way you are moving. Witnessing is the path, and you are starting to feel once in a while a thoughtless moment. These are glimpses of no-mind . . . but just for a moment.

Remember one fundamental law: that which can exist just for a moment can also become eternal. You are given not two moments together, but always one moment. And if you can transform one moment into a thoughtless state, you are learning the secret. Then there is no hindrance, no reason why you cannot change the second moment, which will also come alone, with the same potential and the same capacity.

If you know the secret, you have the master key which can open every moment into a glimpse of no-mind. No-mind is the final stage, when mind disappears forever and the thoughtless gap becomes your intrinsic reality. If these few glimpses are coming, they show you are on the right path and you are using the right method.

But don't be impatient. Existence needs immense patience. The ultimate mysteries are opened only to those who have immense patience.

I am reminded . . .

In old Tibet it was customary, respectful, that every family should contribute to the great experiment of expanding consciousness. So the first child of each family was given to the monasteries to be trained in meditation. Perhaps no country has done such a vast experiment in consciousness.

The destruction of Tibet at the hands of communist China is one of the greatest calamities that could have happened to humanity. It is not only a question of a small country; it is a question of a great experiment that was going on for centuries in Tibet.

The first child in every family was given to the monasteries when he was very small, five or at the most six years old. But Tibet knew that children can learn witnessing better than grown-ups. The grown-ups are already utterly spoiled. The child is innocent and yet the slate of his mind is empty; to teach him emptiness is absolutely easy.

But the entrance of a child into a monastery was very difficult, particularly for a small child. I am reminded of one incident . . . I am telling you only one; there would have been hundreds of incidents like it. It is bound to be so.

A small child, six years old, is leaving. His mother is crying, because life in a monastery for a small child is going to be so arduous. The father tells the child, "Don't look back. It is a question of our family's respectability. Not even once has a child in the whole history of our family ever looked back. Whatever is the test to be given for entrance into the monastery – even if your life is at risk, don't look back. Don't think of me or your mother and her tears.

"We are sending you for the ultimate experiment in human consciousness with great joy, although the separation is painful. But we know you will pass through all the tests; you are our blood, and of course you will keep the dignity of your family."

The small child rides on a horse with a servant riding on another horse. A tremendous desire arises in him when the road turns, just to have a look again back to the family house, its garden. The father must be standing there, the mother must be crying . . . but he remembers that the father has said, "Don't look back."

And he does not look back. With tears in his eyes, he turns with the road. Now he cannot see his house any more, and one never knows how long it will be – perhaps years and years – until he will be able to see his father and mother and his family again.

He reaches the monastery. At the gate of the monastery the abbot meets him, receives him gracefully, as if he is a grown-up, bows down to him as he bows down to the abbot. And the abbot says, "Your first test will be to sit outside the gate with closed eyes, unmoving, unless you are called in."

The small child sits at the gate, outside the gate with closed eyes. Hours pass . . . and he cannot even move. There are flies sitting in his face, but he cannot remove them. It is a question of the dignity that the abbot has shown to him. He does not think any more like a child; so respected, he has to fulfil his family's longing, the abbot's expectations.

The whole day passes, and even other monks in the monastery start feeling sorry for the child. Hungry, thirsty . . . he is simply waiting. They start feeling that the child is small, but has great courage and guts.

Finally, by the time the sun is setting, the whole day has passed, the abbot comes and takes the child in. He says, "You have passed the first test, but there are many more peaks ahead. I respect your patience, being such a small child. You remained unmoving, you did not open your eyes. You did not lose courage, you trusted that whenever the time is right you will be called in."

And then years of training in witnessing. The child was only allowed to see his parents again after perhaps 10 years, 20 years had elapsed. But the criterion was that until he experiences no-mind, he cannot be allowed to see his parents, his family. Once he achieves no-mind, then he can move back into the world. Now there is no problem.

Once a person is in a state of no-mind, nothing can distract him from his being. There is no power bigger than the power of no-mind. No harm can be done to such a person. No attachment, no greed, no jealousy, no anger, nothing can arise in him. No-mind is absolutely a pure sky without any clouds.

You ask, "How does watching lead to no-mind?"

There is an intrinsic law: thoughts don't have their own life. They are parasites; they live on your identifying with them. When you say, "I am angry", you are pouring life energy into anger, because you are getting identified with anger.

But when you say, "I am watching anger flashing on the screen of the mind within me" you are not any more giving any life, any juice, any energy to anger. You will be able to see that because you are not identified, the anger is absolutely impotent, has no impact on you, does not change you, does not affect you. It is absolutely hollow and dead. It will pass on and it will leave the sky clean and the screen of the mind empty.

Slowly, slowly you start getting out of your thoughts. That's the whole process of witnessing and watching. In other words – George Gurdjieff used to call it non-identification – you are no more identifying with your thoughts. You are simply standing aloof and away – indifferent, as if they might be anybody's thoughts. You have broken your connections with them. Only then can you watch them.

Watching needs a certain distance. If you are identified, there is no distance, they are too close. It is as if you are putting the mirror too close to your eyes: you cannot see your face. A certain distance is needed; only then can you see your face in the mirror.

If thoughts are too close to you, you cannot watch. You become impressed and coloured by your thoughts: anger makes you angry, greed makes you greedy, lust makes you lustful, because there is no distance at all. They are so close that you are bound to think that you and your thoughts are one.

Watching destroys this oneness and creates a separation. The more you watch, the bigger is the distance. The bigger the distance, the less energy your thoughts are getting from you. And they don't have any other source of energy. Soon they start dying, disappearing. In these disappearing moments you will have the first glimpses of no-mind.

233

That is what you are experiencing. You say, "I am more and more able to watch my body, my thoughts and feelings, and this feels beautiful." This is just the beginning. Even the beginning is immensely beautiful – just to be on the right path, even without taking a single step, will give you immense joy for no reason at all.

And once you start moving on the right path, your blissfulness, your beautiful experiences are going to become more and more deep, more and more wide, with new nuances, with new flowers, with new fragrances.

You say, "But moments of no thoughts are few and far between." It is a great achievement, because people don't know even a single gap. Their thoughts are always in a rush hour, thoughts upon thoughts, bumper-to-bumper, the line continues, whether you are awake or asleep. What you call your dreams are nothing but thoughts in the form of pictures . . . because the unconscious mind does not know alphabetical languages. There is no school, no training institute which teaches the unconscious language.

The unconscious is very primitive, it is just like a small child. Have you looked at the books of your small children? If you want to teach the child, you have to make a big picture first. So you will see, in children's books, pictures, colourful pictures with very little writing. The child is more interested in the pictures. He is primitive, he understands the language of pictures.

Slowly you make the pictures and the language associated – whenever he sees the mango he knows, "It is a mango." And he starts learning that underneath the picture of the mango there is a certain word describing it. His interest is in the mango, but the word "mango" slowly becomes associated. As the child grows, pictures will become smaller and language will become more. By the time he enters the university, pictures will have disappeared from the book; only language will remain.

By the way, it reminds me to tell you that television has taken humanity back into a primitive stage, because people are again looking at pictures. There is a danger in the future – it is already apparent that people have stopped reading great literature. Who bothers to read, when you can see the film on the TV? This is a dangerous phenomenon, because there are things which cannot be reproduced in pictures. Great literature can be only partially reproduced in pictures. The danger is that people will start forgetting the language and its beauty and its magic, and they will again become primitives, watching the television.

Now the average American is watching television for six hours every day. This is going to destroy something that we have achieved with great difficulty. Now, this person who is watching television for seven and half hours per day . . . you cannot expect him to read Shakespeare, Kalidas, Rabindranath Tagore, Hermann Hesse or Martin Buber or Jean-Paul Sartre. The greater the literature, the less is the possibility of putting it into pictures.

Pictures are colourful, exciting, easy, but they are no comparison to language. The future has to be protected from many things. Computers can destroy people's memory systems, because there will be no need – you can keep a small computer the size of a cigarette packet in your pocket. It contains everything that you will ever need to know. Now there is no need to have your own memory; just push a button and the computer is ready to give you any information you need.

The computer can destroy the whole memory system of humanity that has been developed for centuries with great difficulty. Television can take away all great literature, and the possibility of people like Shelley or Byron being born again in the world. These are great inventions, but nobody has looked at the implications. They will reduce the whole of humanity to retardedness.

What you are feeling is a great indication that you are on the right path. It is always a question for the seeker whether he is moving in the right direction or not. There is no security, no insurance, no guarantee. All the dimensions are open; how are you going to choose the right one?

These are the ways and the criteria of how one has to choose. If you move on any path, any methodology and it brings joy to you, more sensitivity, more watchfulness and gives a feeling of immense well-being – this is the only criterion that you are going on the right path. If you become more miserable, more angry, more egoist, more greedy, more lustful – those are the indications that you are moving on a wrong path.

On the right path your blissfulness is going to grow more and more every day, and your experiences of beautiful feelings will become tremendously psychedelic, more colourful – colours that you have never seen in the world, fragrances that you have never experienced in the world. Then you can walk on the path without any fear that you can go wrong.

These inner experiences will keep you always on the right path. Just remember that if they are growing, that means you are moving. Now you have only a few moments of thoughtlessness . . . It is not a simple attainment; it is a great achievement, because people in their whole lives know not even a single moment when there is no thought.

These gaps will grow.

As you will become more and more centred, more and more watchful, these gaps will start growing bigger. And the day is not far away – if you go on moving without looking back, without going astray – if you keep going straight, the day is not far away when you will feel for the first time that the gaps have become so big that hours pass and not even a single thought arises. Now you are having bigger experiences of no-mind.

The ultimate achievement is when 24 hours a day you are surrounded with no-mind.

That does not mean that you cannot use your mind; that is a fallacy propounded by those who know nothing about no-mind. No-mind does not mean that you cannot use the mind; it simply means that the mind cannot use you.

No-mind does not mean that the mind is destroyed. No-mind simply means that the mind is put aside. You can bring it into action any moment you need to communicate with the world. It will be your servant. Right now it is your master. Even when you are sitting alone it goes on, yakkety-yak, yakkety-yak – and you cannot do anything, you are so utterly helpless.

No-mind simply means that the mind has been put in its right place. As a servant, it is a great instrument; as a master, it is very unfortunate. It is dangerous. It will destroy your whole life.

Mind is only a medium for when you want to communicate with others. But when you are alone, there is no need of the mind. So whenever you want to use it, you can use it.

And remember one thing more: when the mind remains silent for hours, it becomes fresh, young, more creative, more sensitive, rejuvenated through rest.

Ordinary people's minds start somewhere around three or four years of age, and then they go on continuing for 70 years, 80 years without any holiday. Naturally they cannot be very creative. They are utterly tired – and tired with rubbish. Millions of people in the world live without any creativity. Creativity is one of the greatest blissful experiences. But their minds are so tired . . . they are not in a state of overflowing energy.

The man of no-mind keeps the mind in rest, full of energy, immensely sensitive, ready to jump into action the moment it is ordered. It is not a coincidence that the people who have experienced no-mind, their words start having a magic of their own. When they use their mind, it has a charisma, it has a magnetic force. It has tremendous spontaneity and the freshness of the dewdrops in the early morning before the sun rises. And the mind is nature's most evolved medium of expression and creativity.

So the man of meditation – or in other words, the man of no-mind – changes even his prose into poetry. Without any effort, his words become so full of authority that they don't need any arguments. They become their own arguments. The force that they carry becomes a self-evident truth. There is no need for any other support from logic or from scriptures. The words of a man of no-mind have an intrinsic certainty about them. If you are ready to receive and listen, you will feel it in your heart:

The self-evident truth.

Look down the ages: Gautam Buddha has never been contradicted by any of his disciples; neither has Mahavira, nor Moses, nor Jesus. There was something in their very words, in their very presence, that convinced you. Without any effort of converting you, you are converted. None of the great masters have been missionaries; they have never tried to convert anyone, but they have converted millions.

It is a miracle – but the miracle consists of a rested mind, of a mind which is always full of energy and is used only once in a while.

When I speak to you, I have to use the mind. When I am sitting in my room almost the whole day, I forget all about the mind. I am just a pure silence . . . and meanwhile the mind is resting. When I speak to you, those are the only moments when I use the mind. When I am alone, I am utterly alone, and there is no need to use the mind.

You say, "When I hear you say 'Meditation is witnessing', I feel I understand. But when you talk about no-mind, it doesn't sound easy at all."

How can it sound easy? Because it is your future possibility. Meditation you have started; it may be in the beginning stages, but you have a certain experience of it that makes you understand me. But if you can understand meditation, don't be worried at all. Meditation surely leads to no-mind, just as every river moves toward the ocean without any maps, without any guides. Every river without exception finally reaches to the ocean. Every meditation without exception finally reaches to the state of no-mind.

But naturally, when the Ganges is in the Himalayas wandering in the mountains and in the valleys, it has no idea what the ocean is, cannot conceive of the existence of the ocean – but it is moving toward the ocean, because water has the intrinsic capacity of always finding the lowest place. And the oceans are the lowest place . . . so rivers are born on the peaks of the Himalayas and start moving immediately toward lower spaces, and finally they are bound to find the ocean.

Just the reverse is the process of meditation: it moves upwards to higher peaks, and the ultimate peak is no-mind. No-mind is a simple word, but it exactly means enlightenment, liberation, freedom from all bondage, experience of deathlessness and immortality.

Those are big words and I don't want you to be frightened, so I use a simple word: no-mind.

Epilogue

Relax and Enlightenment Comes

Is it possible to become enlightened in a really easy and relaxed way, with not too much effort and lots of naps?

You are asking me, a man who has never done anything. Just through relaxation . . . without any effort and lots of naps! Mostly I am asleep. I just get up to talk to you in the morning, then I go back to sleep; then I get up again in the evening to talk to you and go back to sleep. My total hours of sleep must be 18. Six hours I am awake, two hours with you, one hour for my bath, for my food and the remainder I am in absolute *samadhi*. And I don't even dream – so lazy! And you are asking *me* the question?

This is my whole philosophy, that you should not make any effort, that you should relax and enlightenment comes. It comes when it finds you are really relaxed, no tension, no effort and immediately it showers on you like thousands of flowers.

But all the religions have been teaching just the opposite: that enlightenment is very arduous, it takes life-long efforts, perhaps many lives, and then too there is no certainty, no guarantee. You can lose the way even when you are only one step away from enlightenment. And you don't know the way toward enlightenment! So there is every possibility of losing the way, of going astray. By chance a few people have stumbled upon enlightenment. It was just by accident.

Millions of people have been trying and finding nothing and they are not aware that their very search is making them too tense; their very effort is creating a state in which enlightenment cannot happen. Enlightenment can happen when you are so silent, so relaxed, that you are almost not. Just a pure silence and immediately the explosion, the explosion of your luminous soul.

The people who have been very arduous in their search simply destroyed their intelligence, or their body, and I don't think they attained to enlightenment. The very few people who have attained to enlightenment have attained in a relaxed state. Relaxation is the very soil in which the roses of enlightenment grow.

So it is good that you want to be relaxed, at ease, with no effort and lots of naps. This is the recipe; you will get enlightened. You can get enlightened today! Enlightenment is your innermost being. Just because you are so much engaged in effort, in seeking, in searching, doing this, doing that, you never reach to your own self. In relaxation you are not going anywhere, you are not doing anything and the grass starts growing by itself.

All that is needed is alertness, intelligence, consciousness, which are not efforts; witnessing, watching, which are not tensions. They are very joyful experiences. You don't get tired of them. You get very calm and quiet.

Intelligence has not been known to be a part of your so-called saints. They destroyed it completely by their stupid efforts. And I say unto you, all efforts for enlightenment are stupid.

Enlightenment is your nature! It is just that you don't know, otherwise you are enlightened already. As far as I am concerned you are all enlightened, because I can see your luminous flame within. When I see you, I don't see your figure, I see your being, which is just a beautiful flame.

It is said that Gautam Buddha was surprised that the moment he became enlightened the whole existence became enlightened, because his own eyes changed, his own vision changed. He could look as deep into everyone, even animals and trees, as he could look into himself. He could see that they are all moving toward enlightenment.

Everything needs to realize its own nature. Without that, life is not a joy, not a festivity.

Just be a little intelligent and enlightenment will happen on its own accord; you don't even have to think about it.

A woman walks into a bank and goes to the bank president's office. She walks straight up to his desk and says, "I would like to make a ten-thousand-dollar bet."

"I am sorry, madam," replies the president, "but this bank does not take bets."

"I don't want to bet with the bank," she says, "I want to bet with you. I bet that by ten o'clock tomorrow your testicles will be square."

"I think you are a fool," says the president, "but I will take the bet. Be here at ten tomorrow, and bring ten thousand dollars."

At nine fifty-five, the woman walks in with a tall, stately-looking gentleman. "Who is this guy?" asks the president.

"He is my attorney," replies the woman. "He has come to see that everything is done right."

"Okay," says the president, and laughing he pulls down his pants.

The woman reaches over and feels if they are square. At that moment, the attorney collapses in a dead faint. "What is up with him?" asks the president.

"Well," replies the woman, "I bet him fifty thousand dollars that by ten this morning I would have a bank president by the balls."

Just be a little intelligent!

The manager, looking angry, strides over to Paddy's desk and taps him on the shoulder.

"Listen," he says, "do me and everyone a favour and stop whistling while you work."

"Hey, man," says Paddy, "who is working?"

A cannibal chief treats himself to a Mediterranean cruise, and on the first night he sits down for dinner and asks for the wine list. He orders a bottle of French wine and consumes it immediately. Then the waiter approaches him and asks if he would like to see the menu.

"No thanks," the chief replies. "Just bring me the passenger list."

A Catholic missionary is captured by cannibals and is surprised to find out that the chief has been to school in England and speaks perfect English.

"I can't understand it," says the indignant priest. "How could you have spent so much time in civilization and still eat people?"

"A-ha!" says the chief. "But now I use a knife and fork."

Just be a little intelligent. The world is not intelligent. It is functioning in a very unintelligent way and is creating all kinds of miseries for everyone rather than helping them to be happier. Everybody is pulling on each other's legs, dragging them into deeper darkness, into deeper mud, into deeper trouble. It seems in this world everybody enjoys only one thing, and that is creating misery for others. That's why such a cloud of darkness surrounds the earth. Otherwise there would have been a continuous festival of lights – and not ordinary lights, but lights of your very being.

Why have the priests succeeded in convincing man that enlightenment is a very difficult, almost impossible task? The reason is in your mind. Your mind is always interested in the difficult, in the impossible, because that gives it a challenge and the ego needs challenges to become bigger and bigger and bigger.

The priests were successful in convincing you that enlightenment is very difficult, almost impossible. In millions of people only once in a while does a man become enlightened. Their idea was that you should not become enlightened. To prevent you from enlightenment they used a very clever device. They challenged your ego and you became interested in all kinds of rituals, in all kinds of austerities, self-torture. You made your own life as deep an anguish as possible.

But these people who have made their life a torture, masochists, cannot become enlightened. They go on becoming more and more endarkened. And these people living in darkness start crawling like slaves very easily, because they have lost all their intelligence, all their consciousness in their strange effort.

Have you seen a dog in winter just resting in the sun in the early morning? He sees his tail and immediately becomes interested. What is it? He jumps to catch the tail. But then he becomes crazy, because this seems very strange. As he jumps, the tail also jumps. Yet the distance between the dog and the tail remains the same. He goes round and round. I have watched: the more the tail jumps the more determined he becomes; he uses all his willpower, tries this way and that way to catch hold of it. But the poor dog does not know that it is not possible to catch hold of it. It is already part of him. So when he jumps, it jumps.

Enlightenment is not difficult, not impossible. You don't have to do anything to get it. It is just your intrinsic nature, it is your very subjectivity. All that you have to do is for a moment relax totally, forget all doing, all efforts, so that you are no longer occupied anywhere. This unoccupied consciousness suddenly becomes aware that, "I am it."

Enlightenment is the easiest thing in the world, but the priests never wanted the whole world to become enlightened. Otherwise people would not be Christians, they would not be Catholics, they would not be Hindus, they would not be Mohammedans. They have to be kept unenlightened. They have to be kept blind to their own nature. And they have found a very clever way. They are not to do anything, they have just to give you the idea that it is a very difficult, impossible task.

Your ego became immediately interested. The ego is never interested in the obvious. It is never interested in that which you are. It is only interested in a faraway goal – the further the goal, the greater the interest. But enlightenment is not a goal and it is not even an inch away from you – it is you!

The seeker is the sought.

The observer is the observed.

The knower is the known.

Once you understand that your very nature is enlighten-ment . . . in fact, the Sanskrit word for religion is *dharma*. It means nature, your very nature. It does not mean a church, it does not mean a theology, it simply means your nature. For example, what is the *dharma* of fire? To be hot. And what is the *dharma* of water? To flow downwards. What is the nature of man? What is the *dharma* of man? To become enlightened, to know one's godliness.

If you can understand the easiness, no, effortless achieve-ment of your nature . . . I'll call you intelligent only if you can understand this; if you cannot understand this, you are not intelligent, you are simply an egoist who is trying . . . Just as some egoists are trying to be the richest man, a few other egoists are trying to be the most powerful, a few egoists are trying to become enlightened. But enlightenment is not possible for the ego: riches are possible, power is possible, prestige is possible, and they are difficult things, very difficult.

Henry Ford, one of the richest men of his time though he was born poor, was asked, "What is your desire in the next life?"

He said, "I don't want to be the richest man again. It has been a continuous self-torture my whole life. I have not been able to live. I used to reach the factory early in the morning at seven o'clock, and the manual workers would reach at eight o'clock, the clerks would reach at nine o'clock and the manager would come at ten o'clock and leave at two o'clock; everybody else would leave at five o'clock and I had to work late into the night, sometimes up to ten, sometimes up to twelve.

"I worked hard to become the richest man and I became the richest man. But what is the point? I could not enjoy anything. I worked harder than my labourers. They enjoyed life more. I had no holidays. Even on holidays I used to go to the factory to work out plans for the future."

It is difficult, but you can become the richest man if you make enough effort. It is difficult, but you can reach the top of Everest if you make enough effort. But if you make any effort at all, enlightenment becomes impossible for you. If you bring your mind with all its tensions and worries to work out your enlightenment, you are moving in the wrong direction, away from enlightenment.

You need a total let-go, an utterly peaceful, tensionless, silent state of being. And suddenly . . . the explosion. You are all born enlightened whether you realize it or not.

Society does not want you to realize it. Religions don't want you to realize it. Politicians don't want you to realize it, because it goes against every vested interest. They are living and sucking your blood because you are unenlightened. They are able to reduce the whole of humanity into stupid labels: Christian, Hindu, Mohammedan, as if you are things, commodities. They have labelled on your forehead who you are.

In India you will actually find Brahmins with symbols on their foreheads. You can see the symbol and you can recognize to which class of Brahmin this man belongs. These are means or commodities. They have their symbols marked on their foreheads. You may not have your symbol marked, but you know deep down it is engraved within your being that you are a Christian, that you are a Buddhist, that you are a Hindu.

If you all become enlightened, you will be simply light, a joy to yourself and to others, a blessing to yourself and to the whole of existence, and you will be the ultimate freedom. Nobody can exploit you, nobody can in any way enslave you. And that is the problem: nobody wants you to become enlightened. Unless you see the point you will go on playing into the hands of the vested interests which are all parasites. Their only function is how to suck blood out of you.

If you want freedom, enlightenment is the only freedom. If you want individuality, enlightenment is the only individuality. If you want a life full of blessings, enlightenment is the only experience. And it is very easy, utterly easy; it's the one thing you don't have to do anything to get, because it is already there. You just have to relax and see it.

Hence in India we have nothing parallel to Western philosophy. Philosophy means thinking about truth, 'love of knowledge'. In India what we have is a totally different thing. We call it *darshan*. And *darshan* does not mean thinking, it means *seeing*.

Your truth is not to be thought about, it has to be seen. It is already there. You don't have to go anywhere to find it. You don't have to think about it, you have to stop thinking so that it can surface in your being.

Unoccupied space is needed within you so that the light that is hidden can expand and fill your being. It not only fills your being, it starts radiating from your being. Your whole life becomes a beauty, a beauty that is not of the body, but a beauty that radiates from within, the beauty of your consciousness.

Appendix

About Osho

Osho defies categorization. His thousands of talks cover everything from the individual quest for meaning to the most urgent social and political issues facing society today. Osho's books are not written but are transcribed from audio and video recordings of his extemporaneous talks to international audiences. As he puts it, "So remember: whatever I am saying is not just for you . . . I am talking also for the future generations." Osho has been described by the *Sunday Times* in London as one of the "1000 Makers of the 20th Century" and by American author Tom Robbins as "the most dangerous man since Jesus Christ". *Sunday Mid-Day* (India) has selected Osho as one of ten people – along with Gandhi, Nehru and Buddha – who have changed the destiny of India. About his own work Osho has said that he is helping to create the conditions for the birth of a new kind of human being. He often characterizes this new human being as "Zorba the Buddha" – capable of enjoying both the earthy pleasures of a Zorba the Greek and the silent serenity of a Gautama the Buddha. Running like a thread through all aspects of Osho's talks and meditations is a vision that encompasses both the timeless wisdom of all ages past and the highest potential of today's (and tomorrow's) science and technology. Osho is known for his revolutionary contribution to the science of inner transformation, with an approach to meditation that acknowledges the accelerated pace of contemporary life. His unique OSHO Active Meditations are designed to first release the accumulated stresses of body and mind, so that it is then easier to take an experience of stillness and thought-free relaxation into daily life.

Two autobiographical works by the author are available:

Autobiography of a Spiritually Incorrect Mystic, New York: St Martin's Press, 2000.
Glimpses of a Golden Childhood, India: OSHO Media International.

OSHO International Meditation Resort

Location
Located 100 miles southeast of Mumbai in the thriving modern city of Pune, India, the OSHO International Meditation Resort is a holiday destination with a difference. The Meditation Resort is spread over 28 acres of spectacular gardens in a beautiful tree-lined residential area.

OSHO Meditations
A full daily schedule of meditations for every type of person includes both traditional and revolutionary methods, and particularly the OSHO Active Meditations™. The meditations take place in what may be the world's largest meditation hall, the OSHO Auditorium.

OSHO Multiversity

Individual sessions, courses and workshops cover everything from creative arts to holistic health, personal transformation, relationship and life transition, transforming meditation into a lifestyle for life and work, esoteric sciences, and the "Zen" approach to sports and recreation. The secret of the OSHO Multiversity's success lies in the fact that all its programmes are combined with meditation, supporting the understanding that as human beings we are far more than the sum of our parts.

OSHO Basho Spa

The luxurious Basho Spa provides for leisurely open-air swimming surrounded by trees and tropical green. The uniquely styled, spacious jacuzzi, the saunas, gym, tennis courts . . . all these are enhanced by their stunningly beautiful setting.

Cuisine

A variety of different eating areas serve delicious Western, Asian and Indian vegetarian food – most of it organically grown especially for the Meditation Resort. Breads and cakes are baked in the resort's own bakery.

Nightlife

There are many evening events to choose from – dancing being at the top of the list! Other activities include full-moon meditations beneath the stars, variety shows, music performances and meditations for daily life.

Or you can just enjoy meeting people at the Plaza Café, or walking in the night-time serenity of the gardens of this fairy-tale environment.

Facilities

You can buy all of your basic necessities and toiletries in the Galleria. The OSHO Multimedia Gallery sells a large range of OSHO media products. There is also a bank, a travel agency and a Cyber Café on campus. For those who enjoy shopping, Pune provides all the options, ranging from traditional and ethnic Indian products to all of the global brand-name stores.

Accommodation

You can choose to stay in the elegant rooms of the OSHO Guesthouse, or for longer stays on campus you can select one of the OSHO Living-In programme packages. Additionally there is a plentiful variety of nearby hotels and serviced apartments.

www.osho.com/meditationresort
www.osho.com/guesthouse
www.osho.com/livingin

For more information:

www.OSHO.com

a comprehensive multi-language website including a magazine, OSHO Books, OSHO TALKS in audio and video formats, the OSHO Library text archive in English and Hindi and extensive information about OSHO Meditations. You will also find the programme schedule of the OSHO Multiversity and information about the OSHO International Meditation Resort.

Websites

www.OSHO.com/OSHOtimes
www.OSHO.com/Resort
www.youtube.com/OSHOinternational
www.Twitter.com/OSHO
www.facebook.com/pages/OSHO.International

To contact **OSHO International Foundation:**

www.osho.com/oshointernational,
oshointernational@oshointernational.com

WATKINS

Sharing Wisdom Since
1893

The story of Watkins dates back to 1893, when the scholar of esotericism John Watkins founded a bookshop, inspired by the lament of his friend and teacher Madame Blavatsky that there was nowhere in London to buy books on mysticism, occultism or metaphysics. That moment marked the birth of Watkins, soon to become the home of many of the leading lights of spiritual literature, including Carl Jung, Rudolf Steiner, Alice Bailey and Chögyam Trungpa.

Today, the passion at Watkins Publishing for vigorous questioning is still resolute. Our wide-ranging and stimulating list reflects the development of spiritual thinking and new science over the past 120 years. We remain at the cutting edge, committed to publishing books that change lives.

DISCOVER MORE . . .

Read our blog

Watch and listen to
our authors in action

Sign up to
our mailing list

JOIN IN THE CONVERSATION

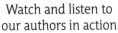 WatkinsPublishing   @watkinswisdom

 watkinsbooks   watkinswisdom   watkins-media

Our books celebrate conscious, passionate, wise and happy living.
Be part of the community by visiting

www.watkinspublishing.com